This book is dedicated to those who would follow Icarus in his self-powered flight but craftily prevent destruction of wings by always falling away from the sun.

Support the U.S. Parachute Team Trust Fund

Because of a special arrangement between the authors and the publisher, every copy of The Art of Freefall Relative Work sold helps support the U.S. Parachute Team.

This happens because the publisher contributes a percentage of each copy's selling price to the U.S. Parachute Team Trust Fund. Authors Pat and Jan Works included this stipulation in their agreement with AeroGraphics.

The Trust Fund was established in 1987 to help provide a permanent source of monetary support to the U.S. Parachute Team. Donations to the the Trust Fund are held in trust forever; the interest they generate are distributed each year to the U.S. Parachute Team that represents the United States in international competition.

As the size of the Trust Fund increases, so will the support it will provide for the team. Eventually it will provide significant financial support.

An important aspect of the Trust Fund is its permanence. As stated above, a donation stays in the fund forever—only the interest the donation generates each year is distributed to the Team.

The Fund is officially recognized by the IRS as a tax-exempt trust; donations to it are tax-deductible in accordance with current law.

The U.S. Parachute Team Trust Fund is administered by the U.S. Parachute Association, 1440 Duke Street, Alexandria, VA 22314.

Contributions to the Trust Fund may be made in any amount and at any time. Simply make the check payable to the "U.S. Parachute Team Trust Fund" and mail it to USPA. You will receive a receipt by return mail.

The organization can also handle any questions you might have about this fund.

Statement of Purpose

Freefall Relative Work

We are a band of brothers, native to the air where we are united in freefall relative work. Our goal is to promote parachuting in general and relative work in particular. RW is a beautiful, exhilarating experience which we like to share with others.

In order to do RW you must relate to others in the air. This relatedness has created a brotherhood of freefall. As brothers we can and should help each other. Because it's OUR sport, we must try to avoid ego-trips, unhealthy politics and hassles. We must promote those aspects of our sport which foster the brotherhood for all.

Good RW promotes itself. RW is where it is today, now. It was non-created. RW just happened and grew. Being non-created, RW is transcendent over acceptance or rejection. Unfettered, it does not ossify into ritual mechanistics and so continues to grow. If directed by a brotherhood of freefallers this growth can strengthen us through unity in numbers. Look how many of us there are today. We are all just beginning. Let's begin together. Do lots of RW.

Pat Works

"Relative Work": (from the French "relatif"): *adj.* relative, relating; *n.* an art practiced by freefall parachutists performed with perfect body and mind control; the movement of the body in the air so that two or more expert relative workers may all fly into various maneuvers such as "star," "snowflake," "wedge" or "bomb-burst funnel"; *syn.* the practice of precision group Skydiving.

In Quest of Perfection...

The Traditions of Freefall Relative Work

1. Our common welfare should come first. Personal satisfaction depends on RW unity: A brotherhood of freefall.
2. There is no central RW authority. Our leaders are trusted servants of the sport; they do not govern.
3. Freefall relative work is democratic and unbiased. The only qualification for membership in the Brotherhood of freefall is a desire to fly for the joy of flying.
4. Each group of RWers has but one primary purpose—to carry the ecstasy and excitement of doing freefall relative work to all parachutists who have enthusiasm for flying.
5. Each RW team or drop zone should be autonomous, except in matters affecting relative work or parachuting as a whole.
6. The Brotherhood of freefall is designed to place principles above personalities and the perfection of flight above all else.
7. The main stem of the Brotherhood is the SCR/SCS awards. The NSCR, 16-man and XX are higher awards.
8. Our relationships with all other parachutists who have yet to join the Brotherhood are based on attraction rather than promotion. The positive results of RW enjoyment, warmth and fellowship emit good vibes which speak louder than any promotion we could possibly do.

Contents

CHAPTER XVI SKYDANCE RESONANCES

MANEUVERS

GLOSSARY

9-cluster   Ray Cottingham

Introduction
Art and Speed

Fast-moving precision freefall relative work is an Art along with music, dance, painting and literature. It is a new Art, and one demanding as much theoretical study, natural flair, learning and practice as any of the classical arts.

It is hoped that you will indulge in the art of relative work to a perfection equal to the highest standard of the maneuver you're attempting. Unfortunately there is sloppy and untidy flying everywhere. Unskilled RW flying in traffic or in the formation is one of the major causes of congestion and small stars.

There is a popular misconception that to be good at relative work, one must fly at top speed and fling the body through the air with little or no idea of what is really going on—speed being the all-important element. When you come to realize that speed is essentially a relative property, mastering the art of relative work will be much easier.

Good, fast, precision RW covers a lot more than going fast; it involves a correct relationship between one's mind and body, and the immensely difficult coordination of the senses with physical movements. Speed itself (relative air speed) is less important than perfecting the basic art of relative work flying. If you perfect the basic art of flying first, an increase in speed will come automatically.

Attention to your basic freefall "stable position" will improve your RW. Practice at performing the basic RW maneuvers will result in a more relaxed approach to doing RW which will automatically be followed by improved concentration and being "fast" as the end product.

As the Elder advised Jonathan Livingston Seagull: "Heaven is being perfect...you will begin to touch heaven, Jonathan, in the moment that you touch perfect speed. And that isn't flying a thousand miles an hour, or a million, or flying at the speed of light. Because any number is a limit, and perfection doesn't have limits. Perfect speed, my son, is being there."[1]

Being good...being fast...being there...comes from subconsciously looking ahead a few tenths of a second earlier than you are used to. You will find that time expands from seconds to much longer. This looking ahead will result in greater relaxation, smoother movements, quicker thinking and reaction, and greater appreciation of the exhilarating beauty of skydiving. Your jerky movements will become smooth movements. You'll learn RW. You'll learn your limits of speed.

Conversely, one of the failings of many a would-be flyer is an inability to go fast—ever. He feels he must always "work his way in." But by doing so, he loses air speed, thus lessening his control!

And so this is a book of techniques for the parachutist who would perfect his freefall flying. It is a book of attitude as well. One of control...and abandon. It is meant to be read and studied as you progress toward perfect freedom of expression in flight. It was written with the understanding that parachutists will forever try their wings to achieve the dreams of flight we've all shared.

This book was written because it needed to be written. People who nurture the desire to fly deserve the input of what has gone before. This book relates the truth as we understand it about the art of flying the body. If applied correctly, this art will return to the reader much more than the reading.

[1]Bach, R., Macmillan, 1970.

Chapter I
Theory of Relative Work

How to Fly on Wings of Wind

This chapter will help you to understand flying your body. If you can't grasp it all at this point, reread it after making 15 or 20 jumps in which you've applied some of this theory.

You Can Fly...In the Same Way an Aircraft Does!

Aircraft are either lighter or heavier than air; blimps and balloons on one hand, and airplanes and rockets on the other.

Descending aircraft of both types use gravity as their "power" in place of their engine. Descending aircraft with power "off" and the human body in freefall perform in much the same manner. The rate of descent in feet per second depends on the angle of attack of the body or aircraft on the wind. For both, a high angle of attack results in a glide (track) while a very low angle of attack is a dive.

Fig. 1 Glide (track).

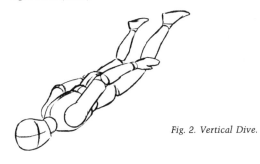

Fig. 2. Vertical Dive.

Both the aircraft and the skydiver's body are controllable in a descent, because both use control surfaces to vary the angle of attack. Both are considered to be flying; just as an airplane in a descent (dive) is not crashing, the skydiver is flying, not falling.

A quote from James Barrie's *Peter Pan:*
One of the high points of the story is when Peter invites Wendy to Never-Never-Land to be storyteller-in-residence:

"Oh dear, I can't. Think of mummy! Besides, I can't fly."

"I'll teach you."

"Oh, how lovely to fly."

"I'll teach you how to jump on the wind's back, and then away we go."

"Oo!" she exclaimed rapturously.

"Wendy, Wendy, when you are sleeping in your silly bed you might be flying about with me saying funny things to the stars."

The wind's back...parlance with constellatory wits ...away we go...suffer, earthbound readers."

...Far out! Lookit...I'm flying!

Flying an Airplane

The aerodynamics of a wing are difficult to understand, tricky to handle. Man has been flying powered aircraft for 70 years, but it's still a difficult art. As parachutists we've been flying our bodies for more than ten years, and it's still just as difficult. This is because in all flight things are often not what they seem to be to our ground-oriented heads. Thus, flying is difficult to learn.

What makes freefall relative work flying so difficult is that the flyer's instincts—his most deeply established habits of mind and body—will tempt him to do exactly the wrong thing. In learning the art of relative work, skills, ideas and habits must be developed where there were none before. In learning the art of RW, much carefully learned behavior and many firmly held ideas must first be forgotten and erased or actually reversed!

It is because of this contrariness to common sense that RW requires "nerve" or full control of the mind. There are many situations in RW when flinching, stiffening up or worrying so as to lose the ability to concentrate will blow the entire jump. And many people who can do RW to the point of entering a star will then blank out and let the formation self-destruct. Or very commonly, beginners will bend over, tense and straighten their legs on entry and bobble, potato-chip or bomb the star. The only recovery from this situation is to RELAX the body and mind. It requires presence of mind, and that isn't easy.

All of this might seem to make learning RW mostly a matter of drill or reflex training, like boxing, judo, fencing, karate, etc. It is. However, there are other routes to learning RW.

It may be that our common sense and our natural reactions mislead us simply because they are working on the basis of wrong ideas in our minds about the body and how it flies. The body is the simplest form of aircraft; it obeys ordinary physical laws. But flying the bold body is new.

RW is done largely with one's imagination. If you have a clear picture of what your body is really doing, can establish its movement realistically, and then orchestrate that movement to the music of the air and relate all that to your brother relative workers, your RW will be effortless and naturally correct.

So if your ideas of "what's what" are correct, you will do RW well. This means we have to take a glance at some Theory of Relative Work.

Theory of Relative Work

The theory of relative work explains how your body is flown without aid of aircraft, open parachute or other devices.

Right now there are thousands of toads who are wishing they could fly. But wishes haven't helped much since Cinderella's Fairy Godmother bounced doing night RW with an elf.

In order to *do* RW, in order to be able to out-fly Jonathan Seagull, to be the Nureyev of the air, or just to get in cleanly without undue mess, you must understand the magic key to doing relative work. The knowledge of it allows you to see what you're doing in technicolor images inside your head. One click unlocks your brain to most of the secrets of the art of flying your body.

In textbooks this magic is confusingly explained under the name of Angle of Attack. Angle of Attack is synonymous with THE theory of RW. If you had only two hours to explain the "how and why" of freefall relative work to a 75-150 jump RW novice, Angle of Attack is what you should explain. According to Wolfgang Langewiesche, "It is almost literally all there is to flight."[2]

Angle of Attack explains vertical dives, the delta, the max-track, mushing, dropping in, flaring, turns, approaches and Z-ing out. It takes the wonder and confusion out of maneuvers like the hand-track or the reverse arch. No RW maneuver can be fully understood without understanding this one thing. While you don't have to know it to do RW, it will help you to learn RW.

You still may be a bit of a clod at swooping; you still may not be able to coordinate your arms, hands, feet, legs and body, but if you understand Angle of Attack, then you'll understand the theory of RW and not be puzzled. You will be able to figure out what you should do. You will be able to analyze your mistakes, and you'll do better each time you try.

Angle of Attack is not an easy thing to understand, however. It is tough to get your gray matter to grasp the initial principles. It is further confused by the fact that your body (fuselage), arms (wings) and feet (rudders) have infinitely variable configurations.

Firstly, angle of attack is NOT the angle which the longitudinal (long part, head to toe) axis of your body makes with the horizon, ground or star; it is NOT the angle at which you aim up or down. Or in other words, it is NOT the "attitude" your body takes to a referent. The distinction is important because you may be head-low and

[2]*Stick and Rudder*, McGraw-Hill, 1972, p. 6.

have a very high angle of attack, for example, during a max-track.

Here it is and it's an idea you'll want to ponder and mull over, talk to yourself and draw diagrams, fly around the room with until it finally sinks into your muddled brain: THE ANGLE OF ATTACK IS THE ANGLE AT WHICH THE EFFECTIVE "WING" SURFACES OF YOUR BODY MEET THE AIR.

You technically-oriented, scholarly types should forget Bernoulli's Theorem…it won't help you do RW. Forget about fluid circulation, too. The key fact of freefall relative work is that THE BODY MOVES BY PUSHING THE AIR AWAY…(re-directing it, if you will).

You deflect the air with your arms, torso and legs. It's really important to understand that your entire body must deflect air in order to move. In exerting a downward or sideways force on the air, you scoot forward or turn or whatever—by the famous old theorem known as Newton's law of action and reaction which makes guns recoil, balls bounce, airplanes fly, etc.

Remember that air is heavy stuff. It weighs about two pounds per cubic yard. Thus, if you fling out an arm as your body swoops through this stuff at over 120 mph, you'll get a hefty reaction.

Deflection of air is what makes a relative worker fly. Newton's law says that if the arm pushes the air, the air will return the push. It's as if you were a piece of 4'x8' plywood and jumped out of a Twin Beech (large door) and while falling you wanted to slide over about 500 yards. All you would have to do is angle down the side of the board in the direction in which you wanted to travel and boogie on over.

Eureka!! In the final analysis, a body in controlled freefall is nothing but a variable air deflector. In flight everybody's RW body is curved and contoured to· be as efficient and effective an inclined plane as we can coordinate it to be. (By the way, the PLANE part of airplane is derived from INCLINED PLANE 'cause that's what it is.)

The body as an inclined plane is what we have to

understand. You incline your body so that as it moves through the air, it will meet the air at an angle and shove it aside in somewhat the same way that the inclined plane of a snowplow, in moving forward against the snow, shoves the snow to the side.

And the angle by which it is inclined—the angle at which you meet the air in order to do a specific RW maneuver—is for every skydiver the most important thing in swooping, for THAT is the Angle of Attack. (Drum roll and trumpet fanfare.)

Go fly yourself and check it out.

To demonstrate to yourself the Angle of Attack, go into a track at terminal. Now visualize the Angle of Attack thing. Imagine your entire body acting as a super air deflector. Feel the force of it. Your toes, shins, thighs, torso, arms and neck should each be doing their best to deflect the air.

Hunch your shoulders forward, pull up your chest, suck in your stomach and tuck your chin in. Put your arms to your sides cupping them downward so that your hands and forearms are really pushing the air. Your legs should be straight, with toes pointed or feet placed 90° sideways. Distance between the legs may vary. If you're doing it right you'll feel a very hefty push against everything.

Push! Watch the ground *move* under you. Grab the material on the legs of your jumpsuit. Really get it on. Imagine yourself to be an eagle or a Phantom jet in a dive after prey.

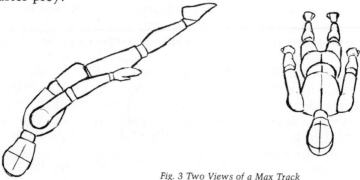

Fig. 3 Two Views of a Max Track

From wingtip to wingtip, your whole body and being should concentrate on achieving maximum deflection of air. You'll feel it when you're there; the speed will exhilarate you.

In this position you have a high Angle of Attack and will cover the most horizontal distance per second.

If you are strong enough you can push too hard and start to stall out into a mush. The drop in speed will be noticeable. In this case you have too high an Angle of Attack. Reduce it and boogie.

Relative Worker, Relative Worker, How Blows the Relative Wind??

Now would you believe an even more realistic picture of what really goes on when we maneuver in freefall? In the demonstration of Angle of Attack, above, we kept things simple. Your angle of attack was rather close to the attitude the longitudinal axis of your body presented to the ground. Or so your head said.

HA! Wrong. Actually the wind wasn't coming straight up from the ground but rather from ahead and below you. Hence the angle of attack cannot be seen simply by looking at the ground or the horizon or the star; **in fact it cannot be seen at all.**

Remember, Angle of Attack is the angle at which the effective wing surfaces of your body meet the air—and we can't see air. That, Bunky, is why RW is an Art. In baseball the batter keeps his eye on the ball he is going to hit. RW is the art of batting the air down with our body as required, but in relative work you can't see the air. Sooo, we often fail to hit it right. We FUBAR up the star and we enter "RW(Attempt)" in our log.

OK, so why not forget it and just keep on trackin' and tryin'? The answer, my friend, is this—if you want to understand RW you must understand the Angle of Attack. Then you have to understand from where, under various conditions of RW maneuvering, comes the air which you are trying to meet and deflect.

When we first started RW, we learned mostly by "monkey see, monkey do" and by asking questions of successful RW'ers on the ground. This mechanical approach at first resulted in several distinct schools of flying around the country. For example, in many cases you can look at a photograph of a star made several years ago and tell in what part of the country it was made by the body configurations of its participants.

Many of these differences in star flying are still with us today. Western jumpers tend to do a more floating kind of RW, using a light, slow-falling base, while in the East or Midwest, the base smokes downward much faster.

This simple difference in the flying speed of the 5-man base makes for vastly different approach techniques and star-flying positions. With a slow-falling star you want to get there quick, grab a "snatch-grip" anywhere between the shoulder and the hand, and then fly the star in a fairly relaxed position. The idea is to keep the base close to the last people out of the plane.

On a smoking base you get there quickly but enter on wrists only and fly in a tight position to keep the star moving fast so the people at the end of the load won't have to slow down to enter.

In either method jumpers are using the Angle of Attack and the Relative Wind to do RW. You could jump with either group by adjusting your Angle of Attack.

What is the "Relative Wind"?

When you ride a motorcycle the wind always blows in your face, right? The same is true of any high speed vehicle. Actually the speed of the vehicle rushing through the air causes the feel of a wind. It's like saying that telephone poles rush by a car. The air doesn't really rush against the motorcycle but the effects are the same as if it did.

This so-called "Relative Wind"—this onrush of air—this "wind of flight" always comes at the jumper from the direction **toward which he is moving.**

Fig. 4. The two bikes moving in opposite directions feel opposite Relative Winds.

While in a dive this Relative Wind comes from ahead and below. If you pull out of a fast vertical dive into a horizontal "swoop," or track, this wind blows from nearly in front of you. While falling stable this wind blows from directly below.

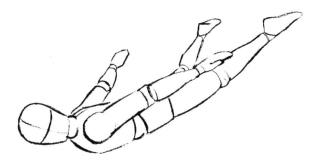

Fig. 5. In a Track. Converting the speed of a dive into a horizontal swoop.

As you do more RW you will practice the side flare and mush and you will develop a sense of your air speed. And importantly, you will develop a feel for the direction of the Relative Wind. You CAN feel it. When an experienced RW'er exits, dives, approaches a star, tracks or flares, he is consciously or unconsciously asking himself all the time, "Where at this moment is the air coming from? And at what angle must my body meet it to do what I want to do?"

Most skydivers will probably deny that they ever think about it. And today most experienced RW'ers don't know the meaning of the words Angle of Attack or Relative Wind. But you can bet your sweet bippy that, subconsciously, most good fliers' minds are on the Relative Wind, although for them it's "feel" rather than deliberate reasoning.

A good relative worker's "feel" for his total body and his almost instinctive ability to handle it right is, on analysis, nothing more than continual awareness of this most important of all flying facts—the Angle of Attack. That is, the angle at which your whole body and its every flying surface meets the Relative Wind.

Think about it. Remember Jonathan Livingston Seagull's words, "As an unlimited idea of freedom, your whole body, from wingtip to wingtip, is nothing more than your thought itself."

Chapter II
Relative Work Maneuvers

Types of RW

There are four types of relative work: terminal, subterminal, momentum and non-momentum. You gotta be good at 'em all.

Non-momentum RW is the kind of RW you learn to do first. You get to within about 30 feet of the dude you want to relate to and are at his level. You stop dead-still and then hand-track over; you have no velocity left over from your descent track.

This type of RW is difficult to do well. Experts at it literally seem to dance on columns of air beneath them. You need to be good at non-momentum RW to enter a squirrelly star or you won't get in. Also, heaven forbid, you might be so fast you go below and the only thing that will get you back up and in is non-momentum RW. On the other hand, if you're going to *be* as fast as you already think you are, then you must be hot at momentum RW, too.

Momentum RW is the kind of RW that builds competition stars. In momentum RW you never stop or slow down; you maintain track-generated velocity and redirect it to enter. You must be very aggressive, and your chances of a wipeout are higher. You generally use the "mush" entry in momentum RW. The "mush" is a high-velocity, sitting-up approach. We'll get into it later.

Relative Fall

Here we want to talk about techniques of performing momentum and non-momentum relative work maneuvers, keeping in mind that the thought behind it all is

Angle of Attack. So all we'll discuss here are maneuvers you do at terminal velocity. Subterminal RW is very specialized because you do not have the flying edge that terminal velocity of 120 mph gives you. The maneuvers are the same, but they must be much more exaggerated and held longer to achieve the same results.

It's unfortunate that students are required to do stable five-second delays before they can progress to longer delays (where they reach terminal velocity and begin to figure it all out.) It's like requiring a student pilot to learn how to do perfect landings and take-offs before you'll teach him to fly.

When you reach terminal, you've reached a relatively constant rate of fall that tends to be uniform with the group you're trying to fly in relation to. Most discrepancies due to body size or mass can be compensated for by jumpsuit or body position.

When many of us think of "falling stable" we usually have as a reference the two positions explained by Russ Gunby[3] as "the basic stable" and the "French Frog".

Fig. 6. Basic Stable.   Fig. 7. French Frog.

[3]*Sport Parachuting*, R. Gunby.

These positions are rather rigid: the arms and legs are held down against the Relative Wind. The idea that rigidity is a necessity in the stable freefall position began to dissolve with the advancement of freefall RW which led to the development of the RW Stable.

The principal idea behind the RW Stable position is that it is not a wind-deflecting position at all. The arms and legs are not held out into the wind to act like outriggers on a canoe for the body, but instead they are consciously allowed to blow back behind the body and provide stabilization like the feathers on a badminton bird or an arrow. The arms and legs and head and torso are brought out of relaxation and into play *only* when movement is desired. The achievement of relaxation in this position requires control and awareness in freefall.

Effective Center of Mass.

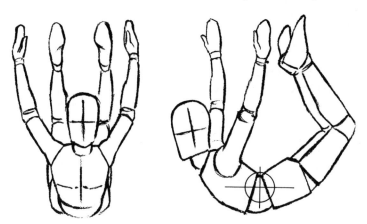

Fig. 8. RW Stable.

All three positions are stable. They vary only in their rate of vertical fall: the RW Stable being the fastest, the Basic Stable being the slowest. The advantage of the RW Stable is its higher rate of "sink" and its stability. This stability is due to a low center of gravity, or effective center of mass. Style-oriented RW'ers lean to the style "tuck" to achieve this same rate of vertical descent. However, for *most* people the style tuck is too unstable in the rough air around a star, where the RW Stable is preferred.

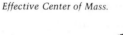

Effective Center of Mass.

Fig. 9. Style Tuck.

When you fall at terminal velocity with a group, your body size or mass may give you a flying advantage or disadvantage over your fellow jumpers. Nevertheless, whatever your size/mass ratio you'll still use the same basic techniques as everybody else. Since your skrawny or rock-like body is a *constant* to you, you'll naturally adjust your body configurations to keep your rate of vertical fall relative to your co-workers. This self-adjustment is probably the basis for the concept of "relative work".

We want to talk about maneuver techniques, so don't let the relative fall thing lead you astray. If you're tall and skinny you have a larger effective "wing" area to use in deflecting the Relative Wind. If you're short and stocky you'll have rather less effective wing area to use. Importantly, although one "floats" while the other "sinks" they both use Angle of Attack to move; and if they are good at it their body size doesn't matter.

Relative Work Maneuvers

You'll use many different modes of motion in RW. There are different modes of moving for specific situations—some are obvious, some are fancy. Consider dives alone: a skydiver may descend in a vertical dive, a vertical no-lift dive, or a delta.

All together I figure there are five major modes of movement: dives, glides, braking, RW turns, and recovery maneuvers.

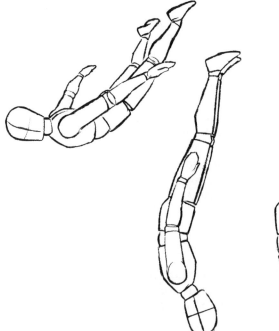

Fig. 10. DELTA—Body has high Angle of Attack and develops considerable lift resulting in horizontal movement.

Fig. 11. VERTICAL DIVE —Body points straight down but flight path is not straight down. Body has some Angle of Attack, some lift.

Fig. 12. NO-LIFT DIVE — Body has no Angle of Attack, no lift. Body is slightly inverted. Flight path is straight down.

The Dives

As noted at the beginning of this chapter, all momentum RW approaches start from a dive and its resulting velocity.

The Delta is the most common dive. In a Delta your arms are back alongside your body and a little bit away from it; your legs are slightly separated and your toes are pointed. Your Angle of Attack is moderately high, resulting in a large deflection of the Relative Wind which is coming from below and slightly ahead of you. The Delta gives a medium horizontal speed and a high descent speed. This dive has some "feel" to it since the Angle of Attack requires some muscle pressure from your whole body.

A word about muscle pressure: as a general rule, relaxed to moderate muscle tension gives you the best control in most maneuvers. Use high muscle tension only when you aren't performing a maneuver with enough speed to get good results.

In the Vertical Dive your body points down. The normal configuration of the body in this position produces some lift. The flight path is not straight down, but forward and down because the body has a slight Angle of Attack. The Relative Wind will come from the direction of movement, or from below and just ahead.

The difference between the Vertical Dive and the No-lift Dive is a changed body position which cancels all lift so that the body seems to "fall" out of the sky. There is no angle of attack. There is no lift. The Relative Wind comes from directly below. You are going downward and fast!

To enter a No-lift Dive start from a Vertical Dive, tuck your chin in and roll your shoulders forward as you bend at the waist. You'll feel your body suddenly fall into the burble created by your head and shoulders. You'll be looking back and up. The position feels distinctly inverted. If you feel the wind hitting the backs of your legs you're a bit too inverted.

In making a transition from a stable position to a no-lift dive, you go from a 90° Angle of Attack (no deflection, high resistance to the Relative Wind) to a 0° Angle of Attack (no deflection, minimum resistance to the Relative Wind), resulting in a speed increase from about 120 MPH to over 200 MPH. That's an increase of about 100%. It is redirection of this dive or track-generated velocity that allows us to do **momentum** RW.

However, the conversion of vertical dive-speed into horizontal approach-speed dramatically changes the direction of the Relative Wind, requiring suitable compensations in Angle of Attack if we are to maneuver well. This conversion is called a "Swoop" and it usually results in a low-angle or level approach on the star. There are other momentum RW approaches which work as well or better; the 45° straight-in and the high approach, but we'll discuss those in the chapter on approaches.

There comes a time in any vertical dive when you must arch out of your high-speed descent and cover the horizontal distance to the star.

This change of direction produces a noticeably increased G-load on your body and a dramatic sensation or "rush." At the same time your body muscles come out of inactivity into a wrenching airstream. The "Swoop" is an appropriate name for the transition from dive to track.

The history of the Swoop is lost in the ozone. We do know that its invention came sometime after Stephan and Joseph Montgolfier made man's first ascent in 1783 in a hot-air balloon. Fable tells us that it was invented by the famed C. G. Godfrog.

THE SWOOP: ITS INVENTION
The Fable of The Godfrogs

ONCE UPON A HAPPEN THERE WAS THIS FROG...Carlos Gene Godfrog by name. "C.G." (as his friends called him) was a clumsy green tree-frog by trade. "C.G." was black-balled by the Tree-Frog Union for "chronic falling out of trees."

Falling out of trees not only hurt C.G.'s body, it hurt his big frog ego, too. Since smarting from a bruised ego is an intellectual process, C.G. was able to figure out a solution to the problem.

It came to him one day whilst he was drowning his Sorrow at the local sleazy Frog Pond. The ravaged Sorrow broke loose to gasp out, "Arrrgh-sputter-SWOOP-gasp-HELP!"

"Eureka!" chortled C.G. as he danced down the nearest yellow brick road to the closest tree. He climbed to the top and began with a slow front loop followed by crushing impact with the ground... C.G. had struck upon the concept of the swoop!

Some 287 tries later he was a mottled red, green and blue, but he doggedly lept on. (Frog watchers take note: this Paisley patterned bruise is the sure sign of the novice God-frog.) Finally his patience was rewarded. Carlos Gene God-frog had perfected the SWOOP!

It happened on the day after Shrove Wednesday in the vacant lot behind Farmer Nasty's barn. From a Dutch Elm (DE-1) from 60 feet, he made a 3-second stable delay and basic spread Swoop impact. Carlos' mastery of his mind and his fear of further damage to his body had given him the internal fortitude to develop a panic flare-arch-roll-your-shoulders forward-and-scream-with-eyes-and-mouth-wide-open technique seldom matched today.

Yes, from these clumsy beginnings, Carlos Gene shot forth into national prominence. Not letting the fame, fortune and bright lights go to his battered head, he modestly bought a yacht, two Twin Beeches, a chopper, a stereo, a van, had his hair processed and a new red, white and blue frogskin suit made.

Shortly thereafter, the Tree-Frog Union arrested, tried, convicted, hung, shot and stomped poor Carlos Gene God-frog for the crime of not being green. He was posthumously elevated to the level of deity of the Neo-American Church where his techniques have been taught in a sanctuary located between 3.5 and 12.5 thousand feet.

Today, as you drive down any street, you may notice very flat, spread-out frogs lying by the roadside. These frogs

*all have the characteristic steamroller-look markings. DO
NOT disturb these frogs. They are novice Swoopers, disciple
Godfrogs who are undergoing a strict fasting and rest period
before attempting their next swoop. They spread themselves
out on the roadside to collect energy from the sun and
warmth from the asphalt. So deep is their trance they can
seldom be aroused except by screaming the sacred mantra
"Pull your reserve, for god's sake!"*

Glides

In its least efficient form, the track is simply a
delta...medium horizontal speed and a fairly high descent
speed. However, the objective of the track is different, the
configuration is different, and the result is different. In a track,
your arms are back, your legs are slightly separated and your
toes are pointed...just as in a delta. But your shoulders are
rolled forward, your waist is bent slightly and your arms press
down with vigor on the Relative Wind.

This results in a high Angle of Attack that produces a
large deflection of the Relative Wind which is coming from
below and ahead of you. It's similar to a ski-jumper's position
with good horizontal speed and a high descent speed. The
track is a medium glide you use to descend and cover a good
bit of horizontal at the same time. It's a glide with a lot of
"feel" due to the muscle action required to obtain the high
Angle of Attack. Most RW'ers feel the track to be the best
method for covering ground...'taint so.

The fastest mode of horizontal RW flying is the max-
track. The max-track is a track modified by the jumper to
produce greater horizontal speed, or more accurately, the
greatest distance of ground covered on the horizontal
plane per foot of fall.   See Fig. 3. page 8.

Since your object is to cover the most ground with the
least descent, the basic track is modified to produce a
much higher Angle of Attack. From the track you roll your
upper torso, head, shoulders and upper arms into an airfoil.
Your lower arms, thighs, and lower legs must deflect a

maximum amount of air. The Relative Wind blows from ahead and below. You do everything you can to cover horizontal distance without losing altitude. Some jumpers grab their jumpsuit leg material to increase the effective size of their Relative Wind deflector.

The difference between a track and a max-track is readily apparent at break-up altitude when everyone separates to dump...those in a max-track will obviously cover more ground than their tracking companions. If you're not physically fatigued after a max-track, you're not doing it right. Compare Fig. 3 to Fig. 5.

The hand track, another glide maneuver, is generally initiated from a stable position. It is the key maneuver of non-momentum relative work. The hand track is probably the "original" RW maneuver because you start from a dead-still stable at level with those you want to relate to, and with no residual velocity left over from your descent track.

From the stable position you bring your forearms and hands down in front of you and hunch your shoulders forward, while at the same time straightening your legs. The angle of attack of your arms, shoulders and legs is very high. The Relative Wind blows from directly below; you use a lot of arm and leg muscles to push down on it. (After a heavy bout of non-momentum RW your pectoral muscles will be sore.)

Fig. 13. Hand Track.

The hand track is used on potato-chipping stars, large-star attempts, after the first maneuver in sequential RW, and in speed-star work whenever traffic or the situation requires it.

The backslide is a kind of reverse track. Use it when your approach is too high or when the formation slides toward you while you are on final approach. When the star is poorly flown or if a person entering the side opposite you floats his side up, the star will rush at you and you can easily get credit for bombing it. When you get rushed by a star you can either turn away and try again, or backslide.

Fig. 14. Backslide.

To perform the backslide, throw your arms out above your head at a high angle. The back is arched slightly and the feet are tucked up out of the way on your ass. Don't let your knees get very far apart. The arms and torso are adjusted to obtain the required rate of backslide versus descent. The rate of descent is high since the legs aren't in use. The angle of attack is controlled by the arms. The Relative Wind comes from below and behind.

If a backslide is entered too abruptly without an adequate arch, a backloop results. This maneuver is called "Z-ing out" and is not allowed, so be careful.

If you're level with the star and it wantonly "attacks" you, the backslide won't help because you'll have a higher descent rate than the star. In other words, the backslide is used generally with a high approach and is considered an advanced maneuver. The backslide differs from a flare in configuration and in objective.

On the other hand, all is not lost if a star at your level "attacks" you while on final approach. You can still get out of its way without losing precious altitude...by flying backwards!

Flying backwards? Yep! The ability to fly backwards often means the difference between getting into a star that is "rushing" you or having to turn and run. You'll have set up your approach only to find that the star is sliding toward you at a rate which exceeds your ability to maintain the proper approach angle for a good entry. If you get too high on the oncoming star, it becomes crashingly easy to end up on someone's back.

Flying backwards enables you to maintain your optimum approach angle. You fly backwards as you descend into your onrushing slot. Obviously this is an advanced relative work maneuver.

Sometimes flying backwards is simply a controlled backslide. For example, you find yourself too high and at the same time too close to the formation to enter cleanly. The formation seems to be eating you up, so to speak. It may even fly underneath you. You can backslide out of the way, and still get in.

Fast sequential RW, such as international four-man, requires that the point man be able to fly backwards. On the Murphy Star, the Diamond and the Caterpillar, for example, a precision point man will backloop, do his 180° turn, and fly backwards toward an area in the center of his teammates designated as the contact area. This maneuver produces the fastest time.

Also, it is impossible to do some of the more advanced alternate and sequential maneuvers, such as the Tri-Bi-Pole in Fig. 15, without having a couple of flyers who can fly in reverse with precision.

Learn to fly backwards, but don't try to learn on a big load. It costs everyone else too much money if your hot-shot RW trick doesn't quite work the first time you try it.

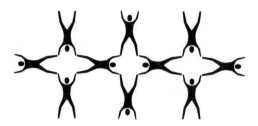

Fig. 15. The Tri-Bipole.

Braking

When you smoke down to an RW maneuver your closing speed is as high as 80-100 MPH. This speed may be all horizontal or a combination of vertical and horizontal, i.e. at an angle. It could also be all vertical. Whichever it is, you have to be able to slow down enough to dock and enter.

You're going a lot faster than the star is because you've reduced your angle of attack and reduced the effective area of your body by presenting less of it to the Relative Wind.

If you used a vertical dive approach and arched out to swoop in on the star from about its level, then your speed has a high horizontal component and the Relative Wind is blowing from ahead of you and slightly below. If you took a 45° dive at the star, the Relative Wind will come from ahead and below. If you did a max-track over to the area directly above the star and then dove down to it in a no-lift dive, the Relative Wind comes from directly below. If you can't feel the real direction of the Relative Wind your braking maneuver, or flare, can't be fully effective and you're wasting time and motion.

Depending on your approach technique, your flare will stop you at wrists or some distance out. In theory, you should dive as long and as fast as you can, brake as hard as you can at the latest possible instant and then smile and enter. That's theory. That's the way you drive a race car, too—go as fast as you can up to a curve, delay braking as long as possible to still be able to make the turn, and press on to victory.

However, you're no race car and the star you're working on is not an inanimate turn. The RW formation you're burning in on is made up of your living friends who may be bouncing around in the star causing it to move about the sky. Imagine how a race driver would feel if the approaching corner moved sideways *and* up and down as he approached it! Imagine how your friends would feel if you used the racing driver approach and muffed it! Imagine how you would feel if you wrecked the star!

Since the star does move, a cool approach is necessary. Leave some flare-power to take care of emergencies. So, while your flare may start out as a body-wrenching, balls-out thriller, you must maintain reserve and FULL control as you near the star. You must know from whence blows the Relative Wind, as mentioned earlier, and you must adjust your flare to the Relative Wind.

The basic flare is a reversed basic stable position, a backward student arch otherwise known as a reverse arch. Chances are that what you believe to be your full-on maximum flare isn't much more than a flat basic stable. Think about it...if you can't see your hands and feet in a flare and if it doesn't hurt, then it's not a full flare, so there.

This "full flare" differs from a "recovery" maneuver in that you are entering from above in a braking flare, while a "recovery" is designed to recover altitude before entering.

To perform a full flare, start from a basic stable and reverse your arch until you can see your hands and feet. Adjust your outstretched arms and legs so that you maintain your desired approach angle. After your full flare you may want to relax your arms and legs into a modified RW Stable to retain control and reserve stopping power.

Sometimes a side-flare is a handy thing to know. The fast, low angle or at-level approach often results in a hard-to-control flare. When you do a vertical dive and swoop out into a hot low-angle approach, the Relative Wind blows from distinctly ahead and below. Most RW'ers using this approach sit up and then flare. As their speed decreases, the direction of the Relative Wind shifts toward below, necessitating constant changes in body position to maintain the proper Angle of Attack. Also, a full flare used with this approach often results in unwanted lift or "ballooning" which is usually countered by bending the legs up out of the Relative Wind's way. This is inefficient because the legs should be used in braking.

An easy way to counter this unwanted "ballooning" problem, which often seems characteristic of low angle approaches, is to lay over on your side and then flare. Said differently, if you can't maintain a low enough approach angle while in a full flare, don't pull in your legs; rather, rotate your body 90° so that it is presented sideways to the star instead of vertical to it. (Of course you'll want to rotate back to enter.)

Knee braking is used to reduce horizontal velocity when the hands are otherwise occupied, as in docking. A fast hand track can be significantly reduced by bringing the knees down to right angles with the torso.

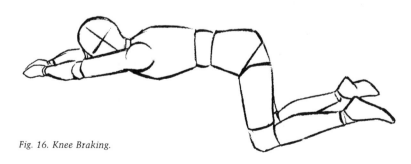

Fig. 16. Knee Braking.

The RW Turn

A look at your logbook will probably show that wiped-out or bombed stars have a fairly common cause of destruction: a skydiver's inability to dock on wrists. If, instead of wrists, he lands on someone's back or legs, problems immediately arise that result in a small star. It happens because he doesn't know how to make an RW turn.

Not knowing how to use the feet and legs to turn while the hands are occupied, not being able to slide with the star as it rotates show a misunderstanding and inability to do the RW turn.

Turning requires constant awareness of your Angle of Attack and of the Relative Wind. It involves using your whole body "from wingtip to wingtip" to move. That means shoulders, head, thighs, legs and feet are all as involved in flying as are hands. And even more so just prior to docking, as the hands are often occupied in targeting in on wrists.

IN ORDER TO MAKE AN RW TURN YOU MUST USE YOUR ENTIRE BODY AS AN EFFECTIVE DEFLECTOR OF THE WIND. This means you don't use "hands only" student turns. You must feel the Relative Wind, see where you want to go inside your mind and adjust your body to get you there.

Use a bank turn to slide off the Relative Wind in a new direction by dropping the side of your body closest to the direction in which you want to travel and raising the other side. In other words, if you wish to turn to the left, make a banking turn by leaning left.

If you want to go sideways or backwards or diagonally, simply adjust the appropriate parts of your body to an angle which will meet the wind to effect the desired change in direction. If you find you're not moving in the direction you want to, then you aren't deflecting enough air to move. Keep adjusting the deflection surface till you do.

Another RW turn that is similar to the bank turn for use close to the star is the "keel turn." Heavier relative workers may find they lose too much altitude with the bank turn. If so, the keel turn may be their answer.

Execute a keel turn by using your inside leg as a keel on which to turn. Draw up the knee to change the direction of your flight as you stop sliding. This works especially well when the star is turning.

Fig. 17. Keel Turn.

Note that these turns are different from student or style turns which effect a simple change in heading. RW turns effect a change in direction of movement.

RW turns should be practiced. It is important to be able to move in any direction without changing heading. Try flying backwards and sideways. Practice no-hands flying to teach your legs to be as effective as your arms.

Finally, don't try to make turns close to the star using only your arms. Make even the slightest change of direction with an RW turn, banking into the turn properly, coordinating your arms, legs and body. It will make that rough entry much smoother!

Recovery Maneuvers

Until you become so good as to never miss; until you join that exclusive 100% club where you're as good as you already think you are, you have to learn how to get back up to where the star is. You have to learn how to go from below those lucky bastards who didn't go low to a level where you can do effective, fully controlled relative work. For when you are below the star you have all you can handle just to get back up.

Recovery requires all of your surface area. You must use every inch of yourself to recover the altitude you need to enter the formation. You'll have no surface left for deflecting wind to approach the star, so you have to do better than "get up" to its level. You have to be able to get up above it again. When you descend you have gravity to assist; you might say that gravity is sort of a motor which you can use to change your speed. The problem in going up is that you have to fight that gravity.

Even when you become a Skygod you'll need to know recovery maneuvers. I've seen flyers who are so used to getting in every formation on the first try, they are at a loss when something unexpected happens and they find themselves below something.

When you want to "GO UP" you must fully concentrate on doing so and put everything else out of your mind. Body configuration is critical. Every inch of you must come effectively into use.

(It is assumed that you will not try to come up in an area where you are a hazard to the star or other jumpers. Should you foul up an RW jump by getting below the star and loitering there, you should letter the words "Stupid Ass" on your forehead.)

After quickly determining that you're not going to come up into a clumsy area, whip into a flat stable and then into the full reverse arch recovery position.

To do this, think aggressively about going UP! Fast! Put some muscle into it! Here's where you use extreme muscle tension. Reverse your body's arch, not just the arch of your legs and arms; reverse the whole thing. Arch your torso. Concentrate on feeling strong wind resistance against all of your body. Get your shoulders into it. You should be able to see both your hands and feet easily. You should be so intensely reverse-arched that you nearly flutter like a falling leaf. Put your feet sideways, heel to heel.

If you do all this and concentrate on it, you'll bob up like a cork. You'll be surprised at the recovery power you'll have.

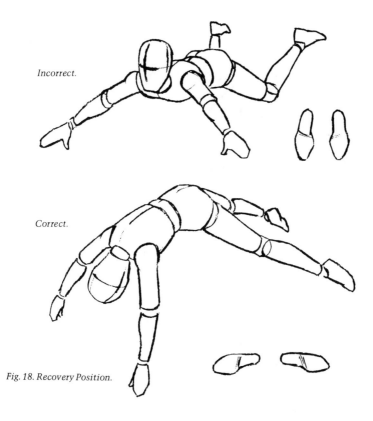

Incorrect.

Correct.

Fig. 18. Recovery Position.

There is a recovery-approach technique that is very advanced but can be learned. It gives you the ability to enter the star from a point below the star (not directly below, of course). Since it's tricky and fraught with hazard, it is ordinarily used as a last resort. Keep it well in mind that it is never okay to selfishly take out a star because *you* want to get in.

To do the recovery-approach you rear-up and use your upper body as the recovery area to cup the air. Your forearms, hands and shins deflect the air and generate some forward speed along with the upward speed. You have to feel for this one.

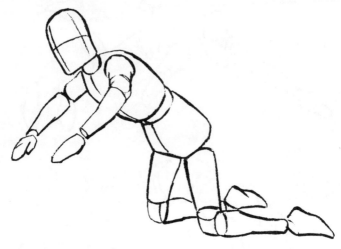

Fig. 19. Recovery—Approach.

RW Across a Vacuum

Sometimes when you're doing "the most perfect final approach the world has ever seen," you'll suddenly find the bottom dropping out. You'll flounder in no air. There is suddenly no buoyant cushion of air for you to work on. You are Falling!

Obviously you've passed over someone below the star, and the vacuum that extends above his back has sucked you down. Or it *will* suck you down unless you react IMMEDIATELY.

Quickly spread all the way out flat and use your hands and feet to creep forward, as in a hand track or recovery-approach. You can probably get out of the vacuum area and perhaps still enter without fully aborting. The trick is to react quickly.

Chapter III
Feeling The Air

 "How I yearn to throw myself into endless space and float above the abyss." Goethe .

Get to know the air you fly in—it's the element of freefall. Air is your friend and official RW helper. It gives you a place to skydive and creates fantastic valleys of clouds for your admiration and company as you engage in the exhilarating aerial ballet of relative work.

Touch the air; it can be warm or freezing. Feel it; it can be so soft as to offer no resistance at all or so hard you can hardly stick your arm out in it. Perhaps strangest of all, it's usually blue except on close examination when it's clear (none of this is true in a smog bank).

Hear it. Inside a conch shell it sounds like the sea. In freefall it sounds like the furies of Hell.

Fly on it. Icarus did; you can, too. Next time you swoop, feel the air. It gets thicker and thinner as you perform RW in the sky. In a dive, when you're going fast, it's very thick. During subterminal RW, it seems very thin.

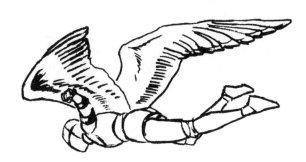

Fig. 20. Icarus.

Air is enlightened water. Buddha said that the One Mind is like the sky. The sky is the somewhat mysterious something you sense when you do freefall. Sometimes you ride the wind. Sometimes you fall like a toad. Feeling the air helps you to ride the wind.

Remember that rocks merely fall while seagulls, stunt planes and skydivers descend. Your flying ability depends on your speed in the air. Your ability to do RW well depends on your awareness of the Relative Wind and your sensing of speed through the Relative Wind instant by instant as you dance toward the formation.

As you feel the wind and test the firmness of the air, you'll change the Angle of Attack of your hand, your leg, or your whole body so that it follows the scenario of your mind. You'll feel it and at the same time you'll notice the effects your movements have on the relative position of your target formation. You'll do all of this with full-on concentration of mind and controlled relaxation of body …and your every thought will be motion.

Air is like water—you can feel its buoyancy. Your skydiving air is "customized" to you and you can make it as thick or as thin as you wish in order to vary your buoyancy so that you can dive through and maneuver in it at will, just as you can in a pool of water.

This varying of buoyancy is keyed by relaxing your star-crazed mind so that your tactile sense of feel can find the direction and speed of the Relative Wind.

The Mechanics of Feeling the Air

The mechanics of feeling the air's buoyancy are simple if you already know how. Otherwise, it's difficult to get into because it is so subtle. It's rather like smoking pot—people seldom get high on their first experience because they look for some striking, obvious effect on the mind and body, a sort of drunken stupor. If the search for these non-existent effects is intense enough, the real but vastly more subtle effects of the weed are overlooked. To enjoy, you have to relax your mind and let your senses relay their messages.

In freefall it's noisy and confusing. The noise, the loss of an unmoving reference as a guide to your movement, the vertigo...all of these things send booming messages into your brain which demand immediate attention.

Result? All you seem to feel is the sound and the fury. You're very much a stranger in a strange land. Your over-loaded mind and senses can't sort out the confusion, can't rank the incoming messages in any order of importance to flying, and you figuratively blow a fuse, just like any other over-loaded circuit.

I've trained hundreds of students and have seen it happen often. They step out into the blinding sky with its hurricane wind and ever-shifting ground; they watch the plane fall up and BUZZzzzap! they go blank.

As you make more and more jumps you become more of a "native" to the sky. You realize that the sound and the fury are nothing more nor less than the neon lights, con-gested traffic, swirling crowds and hustle-bustle of any downtown street. Just as you learn to disregard the dis-tracting sights and sounds of a busy city so that you may notice when the traffic light turns from red to green and allows you to safely maneuver to your destination, you have to learn to do the same thing with relative work.

If you filter out the extraneous messages and react only to those signals which help you do RW, you'll be less confused, more relaxed and "better." You will quit spend-ing your limited time and energy on distractions and thus have that much more time and energy for Swoopin'.

The important thing about buoyancy is that it can be sensed. As noted above, this is one of the more hard-to-get-at skills in the whole art of flying—this sensing of "lift," the gauging of the firmness or "substance" of the air. The "feel" you must have to make contact, and the ability to know what your body is actually doing: this we'll call the flying instinct.

The RW'er needs this sense of buoyancy during al-most every second of every maneuver. He needs it every time he makes an approach on a formation. How many times have you flared only to find that you were too high and had to try to pick up speed again? How many times have you flared too late and had to circle the star, or go below? Your RW ability depends in large measure upon your ability to sense lift or the loss of it. Most spastic "FUBARS" happen only because the relative worker's sense of buoyancy failed him.

The novice RW'er realizes all of this in a vague way. He knows that he needs this sense and he also knows that he doesn't have it. He feels like a blind man walking in traffic.

A vague feeling of frustration plagues the novice. He feels that something important is being left unsaid; that there is some answer, which if given, would help him over the hump. Unfortunately he has little, if any, orientation; he can't ask the right questions. And even if he did, very few would know how to help him.

We will try to help.

One important cue is speed. The sensing of the air's firmness is almost the same thing as speed. Fast flight means flight at a low angle of attack (steep dives) while slow flight usually means flight at a high angle of attack (handtracking.) Speed equals buoyancy, but speed is difficult to judge.

Air can't be seen, so air speed is difficult to detect except in relation to the freefall formation you're working on. Since it's hard to "see" speed you must enlist your other senses to help your eyes.

A good speed cue in RW is the sound of flight. Sub-terminal RW in "soft" air is quiet. A full-tilt, no-lift vertical dive is noisy. Even the unskilled ear of the beginning swooper can easily hear and interpret the sounds of flight. Often, however, he doesn't pay attention.

As Langewiesche[4] says, learning to fly largely consists of not developing new senses, but learning to use your old senses for new and different purposes. Particularly, you must get away from the domination of your eyes and make much heavier use of your hearing, your sense of touch, and your inner ear with its feel for acceleration and balance.

Whether your arms and legs experience a hard or soft

[4] *Stick and Rudder*, p. 59.

feel is an excellent clue to airspeed. In a fast dive, the strength required to stick an arm or leg into the airstream is considerable and you need only expose a small portion to the windblast to obtain a considerable reaction. In sub-terminal relative work you'd probably need to use your entire body in exaggerated movement to obtain a like result.

Most RW'ers are aware of this varying feeling of pressure on their arms; many experienced RW'ers feel it on their legs, too. The best RW'ers feel changes in pressure, buoyancy and speed with their feet, ankles, shins, thighs, pelvis, upper and lower torso, shoulders, arms, hands and head. The desirability of getting full available feel has led to the use of tennis shoes, thin or no gloves, and soft helmets among some relative workers—all for better feel of the air.

Testing the Cushion

Accurate sensing of one's buoyancy is especially important during final approach and docking in the star, particularly if the approach is on a squirrelly or poorly flown star. The RW flyer then seeks just exactly the right amount of buoyancy and horizontal movement. A slight reserve of lift is necessary so that when he arrives at the star he will be able to flare, check his descent, and have just enough reserve buoyancy to cope with a moving star.

How to have exactly the right amount of buoyancy to take care of such a situation? It involves knowing whether you have a cushion of reserve lift, whether the final flare before docking will result in enough lift to check your approach, or whether you will overamp and go below. The best way to find out is to test your flare just a tad early and watch how you and the star behave. You must judge the effect not only by eye, but by kinesthesia with every muscle and tendon. Note the small changes in your weight, the feelings of lightness or heaviness of pressure, and your angle of closure with the star...these are all clues to your buoyancy.

Your perception of balance and relative speed is very

sensitive—provided you pay attention to them. A large part of the art of flying consists of paying attention to the seemingly odd things that really do matter.

Skydivers "feel" for lift almost continuously during their final approach—especially in the last stages where their coast or glide blends into the actual docking.

Try out each of these clues separately. Remember, there is a great difference between merely perceiving something with your senses and **noticing** it. In the situation given earlier, a jungle-dwelling primitive transplanted to an American city street would see traffic lights just as you do—maybe even better. But he would probably overlook them and watch instead the flashing neon signs, pretty store windows and other more impressive things that are much less important than the traffic light.

We see the traffic signs even while thinking of something else because we watch for them and we understand their meaning instantly. We know that, though they are not very attention-catching, they are important.

"The clues by which we fly, the things our senses must pick up in order to enable us to fly, are all perfectly plain, and can be easily and plainly perceived by eyes, ears and so forth, of less than average keenness. Our difficulty in learning to (do RW) is not sense perception, but interpretation of what our senses perceive. We tend to pay attention to the wrong things; we miss the things that matter because we aren't looking for them, because we do not know what they mean."[5]

The process of learning RW would be quicker and surer if novice RW'ers knew more clearly what to watch for. Experienced RW'ers should take time to point out more precisely just what it is the student is supposed to learn. Sometimes it's a clearer idea of the mechanics of flight that is needed. Sometimes it's a clearer idea of what his own body is actually doing. We must teach our students to use their fine senses when learning RW.

Show a student RW'er what the clues are and why they are important, and he won't be such a toad. Once his attention has dwelled on them a few times they become

[5]*Stick and Rudder*, p. 72.

much more noticeable; once the correct response to them has been **practiced** formally a few times, it becomes almost automatic. And that is all the so-called "flying instinct" consists of: small clues, understood correctly, and reacted to automatically.

Stability

Stability is such a basic part of freefall RW it hardly seems worth mentioning, but we'd better.

Everybody who does relative work can fall stable, of course. Are you sure? Stability is more than just going into the student arch and not spinning. Stability in RW connotes the ability to maintain control throughout the entire freefall sequence.

Can you always maintain stability without bobbing in a hard dive? Do all your transfers from dives to approaches come off smoothly with never a washout? If you occasionally do have a momentary stability problem, you will soon solve it yourself. But you will solve it a lot sooner if you think out "stability" before jumping. Importantly, you will be more relaxed as you learn the other so-called "critical" RW maneuvers.

One of the positions that lends itself to smooth RW maneuver transitions is the relaxed RW Stable which was explained under maneuvers in Chapter II. The reason this position is so stable is simple ... you aren't doing anything to mess it up. You perfect it by doing less.

The whole objective of the RW Stable is to give you a base maneuver with a vertical speed you can vary at will to make a transition into another RW maneuver without undue gymnastics. The method is simply to totally relax your body so that your arms and legs blow behind you in the wind. You relax your hands and feet so they are limp and don't induce any turns. You relax your back and shoulders; you let your head blow back. You are fully "resting" on the wind.

The RW Stable position is worth learning. Don't forget to notice the color of the sky, or the rush of a puffy cloud while you're learning it. Or better yet, go up with a friend and learn it together.

It's nice to give yourself fully to the wind—and then work it gently as it tells you its endless story.

Using the Relative Wind on Exit.   Pat Works.

Chapter IV
What It Means to Fly

 When you go up into the air you lose your connection with the solid ground and its comfortable, constant visual indicators of speed and movement—things like the lines on the highway, passing fenceposts and trees, etc. These provide ready reference points that are generally unchanging. Leave these familiar earth-bound surroundings where the only directions you need worry about are right and left, forward and backward, and things are apt to get confusing.

In RW you can fly in an up-and-down sense as well as in a right-and-left sense. There are no familiar visual landmarks to tell you much about your movement. What makes it most confusing is that you are trying to connect with another object also falling in this unmarked, undifferentiated void.

I can't think of another sport like it. In motor racing, the corners stay put as you approach them. In tennis, the ground and the net stay in the same place to give you visual clues to your position and movement. Relative work lacks these clues.

In RW the relationship of the horizon and the formation does give you a rough clue of where you are. If the horizon is well above the star, then you are well above the star. If the horizon is below it, then so are you.

A better indicator is the shape of the star or formation. If you are above it you can see clearly everyone's backs; if you are at a 45° angle to it you will see some backs and some faces. If you are level, you'll see sides of legs within a narrow angle of view, and if you are below the star you'll see stomachs.

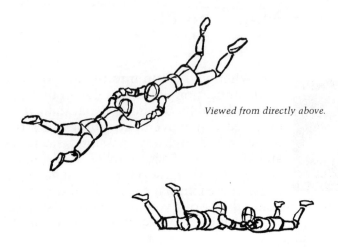

Viewed from directly above.

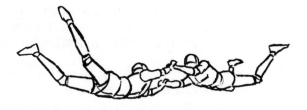

Viewed from at level.

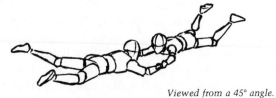

Viewed from below (hopefully seldom!).

Viewed from a 45° angle.

Fig. 21.

Another confusing element when you're approaching a star is the relationship between your height above the formation, your speed and the required maneuver necessary to approach and dock to enter. (This is covered more fully in the chapter on approaches.)

Here is where the visual clues described earlier are tied into your feel of the Relative Wind. It sounds complex, and is. But so is catching a ball, driving a car or any other physical activity requiring motor coordination. What is hard about RW is not this complexity, because your mind can easily deal with far more complex situations, but your unfamiliarity with the situation. You don't know which clues to react to, so you try to "think it out" while you are trying to *do* it. Trial and error plus understanding (and lots of jumps) eventually show the best way and you reach your goal. It's like learning to catch a ball.

When you fly, concentrate on perfection in flying rather than on reaching a goal such as "getting in fast," and you will do better. Relax your mind so that it can receive the sensations of flying which will key the correct response.

Pay particular attention to the size and shape of the RW formation. It will provide your mind with the required data.

If you have trouble docking—if you can get very close but just don't have enough steam to get onto wrists, or conversely, if you're hitting too hard—then you are not controlling your speed. Either you lack enough momentum to dock properly, or you have too much momentum and are endangering the formation. If you can't hit wrists but wind up on legs or backs, see the discussion of RW turns in the chapter on maneuvers.

There are two ways to gain speed. First, you can start out high and convert your altitude into speed: the steeper and farther you go down, the more speed you pick up. At the level of the formation you convert this downward speed into enough horizontal speed to dock. (This is momentum RW.) Or, you can start at-level with the star and hand-track toward it. Here your speed is generated by redirecting the wind.

Both of these methods require feeling the Relative Wind and reacting to its signals while at the same time concentrating on the size and shape of the RW formation. Changes in its size and shape are indicators of your relative position and speed. You must also watch for the formation's relative movement. Since it probably won't stay put you must continually compensate by going toward the spot where it is going to be when you get there.

All of this is what makes the final approach and docking-entry seem so difficult. I maintain that attention to and perfection of the basic RW maneuvers will make approaches and docking almost easy.

Approaches simply show up flaws in your basic RW technique—flaws that otherwise go undetected. If your mastery of flight is firm enough you'll have little trouble with the "advanced" RW techniques. If you really know how to fly an RW turn and how to fly at various angles of attack, you are probably good at RW.

"Hard" vs. "Soft" RW

In momentum RW, you never stop or overly slow down your approach until entry. This redirection of track/descent-generated velocity is controlled largely by your mental attitude and "set." Your actions are choreographed by your imagination and you fly with the "power center" in the middle of your stomach. All of which is a constant for you, but varies between jumpers as individuals. (More on this "power center" later.)

There are various ways of approaching the subject of momentum relative work. Likewise, there are two different schools of karate: "hard" or "soft." In "hard" karate, a powerful direction of energy is used to achieve the desired result. In "soft" karate, the desired result is achieved by redirecting the energy of the onslaught. Relative work uses these "hard" and "soft" definitions in much the same way.

An example of "hard" RW would be the hard flare against the propwash on exit, a strong and furious blind-dive and arch-out swoop at the rushing star, with a balls-out, gut-wrenching flare that puts you on wrists with a snatch-grip to enter immediately.

In "soft" RW you exit, feel the propwash, and flare against its push to a head-high, directly-at-the-star delta. Your chest is held high for lift. Your swoop seems gentle but you keep on cooking in, and your sit-up is only for the entry.

The difference? In hard RW you go faster from exit to flare point. In soft RW you go slower from exit point to flare point, but your time from exit to entry is averagely equal to the "hard" approach. Some prefer this soft RW because if approached correctly, it eliminates personal mistakes even when the star is floating or moving. Hard RW, on the other hand, feels faster.

Again, execution of any kind of relative work requires mastery of all the basic modes of flight as a minimum. This mastery is doubly important. First, it gives you the physical ability and coordination required to perform the maneuvers, and secondly, it gives you the mental confidence in this ability to single-pointedly enter into flight for the joy of flying. When you look at it like that, how can the result be other than satisfying?

Although complete mastery of RW techniques requires effort, it will happen. For in addition to the released energy of your own efforts, you are further assisted by the energy flow from everyone else in the formation who, because you are on the load with them, want you to do well.

Here, then, is the likely cause of much bad flying by experienced jumpers: it originates within their own mind. Everyone in any true sport faces this challenge. The best solution to it is to have the relaxed but attentive attitude of a sharp-eyed eagle diving for slow-moving prey in a vast expanse of ether. SWOOOOP!!! Dinner is served!

Take advantage of our musically-oriented generation. Listen to the music you like. Let your mind's eye hear the symphony, or the rock music, and let your imagination fly as the pertinent signals come in. In the same way, let your mind's eye receive the pertinent signals of relative work. Dig the colors of the formation, the movement and the flash of blue sky.

Multi-person RW sometimes leaks an over-abundance of Ego and fear of poor self-performance. What's needed is reassertion of your true purpose for doing relative work...JOY!

Worrying about what will happen "if," and lamenting what did happen "then," are indulgences. "If" is the Future. "Then" is the Past. Only the act of RW is now. Do RW in the Present.

Fly to the Tune of Your Senses

To enter a star smoothly you must be relaxed with your body, aggressive with your mind, controlled by your will. Skydiving requires precise control of the body. Making it do what you will it to do *when* you will it to happen; knowing where your feet, arms, head and other parts of the body are at all times.

The mind must be controlled at the same time. The mind is a sophisticated sense reader telling you what your body feels and sees. Uncontrolled, it dwells on tension or fear of making a mistake or other destructive thoughts. Destructive thoughts they are, because they take away some of the attention and mental energy of the mind.

If you are to properly coordinate mind and body into precision relative work you must have all your mental energy directed toward one goal: the exhilarating perfection of an art.

In relative work you use your senses—touch, "feeling" the air, sight, sound—all feed data to your mind. Your mind sorts and correctly analyzes this data and the resulting action is more perfect flight.

The mind should be single-pointed so that all the subtle and uncommon sense signals of RW may be received and read. Do not clutter up your flying with fear, tension, ego or pride. Use your will to direct your mind toward performing each movement well. All of the movements, properly performed, will result in superior

RW. Speed will come after ability and skill. Being close does not count; only being THERE fulfills the task.

RW'ers naturally tend to stay in good physical shape; few good RW'ers are flabby and out of condition. Dancing, tennis, skiing and other recreations will sharpen your reactions and senses; disciplines such as yoga and karate improve the will as well. Can you balance on one foot? Can you dance smoothly without looking spastic? Why not?

If the advancement of RW skills through the use of the will to control the mind and body sounds rather mysterious, then let's look at it another way: mental attitude. A good mental attitude helps your flying. A good mental attitude is one that dotes on the beauty of the air—its colors and clouds. A good mental attitude is luxuriating in the dancing, sinewy movements of RW which, in perfection, are pleasure and beauty in themselves. A good mental attitude is a joyful swoop and rush on the star. This attitude toward doing what you love to do helps you to be good at that endeavor because it leaves the mind in a receptive state for reading the many subtle but important messages that instrument freefall relative work.

Myself, I try to dig the beauty of the sky and clouds as we line up to exit. On exit I imagine myself dancing to the music of the wind and savor each movement for its pleasure and expression. It works.

Another friend becomes in his mind's eye an eagle. Another becomes a ballet dancer, another a seagull, others just go to it. The positive attitude is what is important. **You can do RW if you only let yourself do it.**

Red is a friend of mine who digs RW. Once I overheard him talking to some RW novices:

"Some day it's gonna happen to you. I'm telling it like it is... someday you're going to enter the star and you'll feel the electricity that runs through it. It'll blow your mind! Everybody'll be diggin' it just like you do and you'll be able to feel it. I know; it happens all the time."

Final Approach.   Andy Keech.

Chapter V
Approaches

The Descent Approaches
There are three basic approach angles from the aircraft to the star used in momentum RW. There are really two categories of approaches: 1) the descent approach, and 2) the docking or final approach.

The first is used from exit until you set up on final to dock; the second is the final attack technique you use to smoothly enter the star. Note that what the jumper thinks is happening on any of the descent approaches is often contrary to what is actually happening. In any exit you retain the momentum of the aircraft. This built-in speed of 80-100 knots carries you horizontally along with the aircraft until it is dissipated.

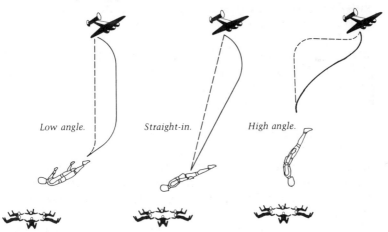

Low angle.   Straight-in.   High angle.

Fig. 22. Descent Approaches.
   What he thinks he is doing. — — — —
   What he is actually doing. —————

Thus, after exit, while your vertical descent remains constant your horizontal speed toward the star will vary with the speed of the airplane and your recognition of this momentum effect. Importantly, for the first 1-6 seconds after exit the Relative Wind blows distinctly from the direction in which the aircraft is moving, miscalled the "prop wash" effect. Remember this.

In the low-angle descent approach you exit and go into a vertical or no-lift dive for 7-9 seconds; then you arch into a delta and swoop in on the star until you reach your flare point. At the flare point you throw out all your laundry to reduce your closing speed and then come in on final to dock and enter. You'll probably want to use the side-flare for the best braking effect.

The flare point and amount of flare is important but the amount of time in the vertical dive is more so. If you dive too long you'll find yourself way below the star (and even if you get in, your approach from below will likely take out someone behind you who falls into your vacuum.) Coming out of the dive too soon wastes time, too. If you use a low-angle descent approach, take these variables into consideration.

Also, in a hot level-with-the-star approach in the sitting-up "mush" position, it's possible to stall out and fall off the air if your horizontal speed gets low and you fail to correct for it by adapting to the downward shifting change in the Relative Wind. Stalls are avoided by your constant awareness of changes in the Relative Wind.

A "mush" is a braking position in which you descend on the star, your body presented at an angle to it. Often after flaring you'll have both vertical and horizontal velocity remaining from your descent dive. You fly in the mush position to compensate for the resulting Relative Wind angles.

The 45° or straight-in approach means what it says. Your purpose is to go from the airplane door to the star in as straight a line as possible. You exit and immediately head for the star, keeping your eye on it and boogie as fast as you can.

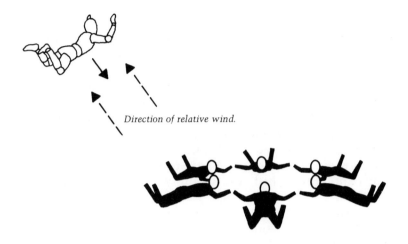

Direction of relative wind.

Fig. 23. "Mush" position.

Your flare will be a little easier to handle than with the low-angle approach, probably due in part to a lower approach speed. But mainly a flare from a 45° descent approach is easier because there is little shift in the direction of the Relative Wind as your velocity decreases. A mush is also commonly used with this approach.

The high-angle approach is the reverse of the low-angle approach. You exit and first concentrate on killing all aircraft-generated momentum before heading for the area way above the top of the star in a max-track. Your purpose is to cover maximum horizontal distance first.

As you approach the area way above the top of the star, bend at the waist and do a vertical dive. Your approach speed on the star will be fast and scary. When you flare, however, you can do a full flare with few complications.

In the high-angle approach, the Relative Wind's direction stays more or less constantly below you (instead of shifting from ahead and below to below, as in the low-angle approach.) However, high-angle approaches must level out close to the star or mishaps are likely. You must also remember that you retain forward motion from the initial max-track. Your dive should be a tad short of the star, or this leftover speed will put you too close.

In each of the above approaches there is a point *outside* the star, somewhere from knees to 30 feet out, where your descent approach ends and you start your final approach to dock and enter. Where this point is depends on your experience, skill, and where your head is.

With the low-angle approach you are more or less committed to a point outside a particular quadrant of the star. With the 45° you can opt for any slot on your half of the star and still get a "straight-in" final. Using the high-angle approach you can pick a spot anywhere around the star during your dive or flare without causing traffic problems. However, there's a chance that someone may move in under you on a lower approach and cause problems for you.

★   ★   ★   ★   ★   ★   ★   ★

Mirror, Mirror, watch my fall.
Tell me please,
The best approach of them all?

Which is the best descent approach for you? Good question. All are used by some very fast people. There doesn't seem to be any standard correlation between body size/weight and the descent approach technique to be used, though some generalizations can be made.

For going early out of a small-door airplane (slots 3 thru 6) the 45° is very good. The 45° approach is also used by some very consistently fast people. The low-angle approach is the oldest and "most natural" but it is hard to flare with. The high-angle approach is fast but scary; you may need to be a low-mass floater type to use it well.

Large-door aircraft in conjunction with a *fast* exit

seem to require the 45° or the high-angle descent approach. Speed isn't desired here because the exit is so fast. The problem is NOT getting there fast. You are already there!—in a big gob with ten other people. The problem then becomes traffic jams and fast entries. Horizontal distance is shorter, the base is much closer and you usually don't have time to build up the speed required for a fast low-angle approach.

Out of small-door aircraft, your exit is spread out and you can opt for any of the approaches. I think the classic low-angle approach is the easiest to start with but it demands a considerable amount of finesse as you approach your limit.

The 45° is initially a bit harder to master but seems to be very consistent. The newest approach, the high-angle, really hasn't been tested yet. It offers several theoretical advantages in the area of control but is difficult for novices to work with.

You can practice any of these approaches out of nearly any aircraft you can do RW out of. If you're jumping a C-182 and want to simulate going tenth out of a small door Twin Beech, just wait 4 seconds after everyone else leaves. Then go and learn your thing.

The Final Approach

After a few fast approaches on a star, the novice RW'er soon realizes how difficult flying into a star can be. Your body has a perverse way of not going where you are trying to make it go.

Actually all of the RW maneuvers are hard to do precisely, but most of them are performed well away from any reference point so that the sorry lack of control we have does not show up as clearly. The final approach, however, takes you out of those empty spaces of air and puts you close to other descending skydivers near the small target of wrists. When you first start trying to hit your target, it's easy to overshoot or undershoot by a wide margin.

The difficulties of the final approach are twofold. One

is the problem of depth perception—the inexperienced eye cannot gauge exactly where the body is going. The other difficulty is a problem of control—in an approach maneuver what you must get your body to do in order to get in often seems directly contrary to "common sense."

For example, as you approach wrists in momentum RW and see that you are going to miss, you will take the corrective action that seems "natural." If you're going to overshoot you will "naturally" want to dive downward toward wrists. But this natural reaction will only make you overshoot still more because it mainly serves to speed up your rate of horizontal movement and thus carry you over the top of the star, much to your confusion.

What you should do in this situation seems counter to your common sense, but it works. A flare and backslide will cause your body to fall more vertically, thus reducing your horizontal speed.

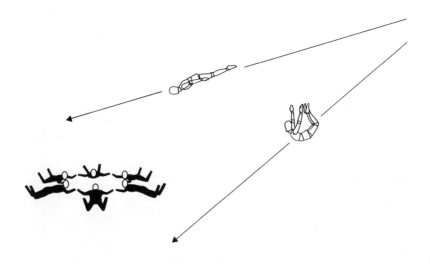

Fig. 24. Momentum RW Final Approach. If you want to come down more steeply, use an RW Stable or a backslide. If you want to come down less steeply, max-track.

You must understand how your approach can be controlled. It's simple. In momentum RW, when you are close to the star and want to go down more steeply, either flare your arms and tuck your legs to backslide, or relax into the RW Stable. If you want to go down less steeply because you are going to undershoot, put your arms back and assume the max-track position.

All of this runs contrary to one's experience with automobiles, sleds, boats and other ground vehicles. And since it is contrary to past experience, it's hard to do the right thing when the time comes. But if you think about it, it does make sense. If you understand the reasons why, it won't be so hard to do.

When practicing final approaches, use the same angle and rate of speed each time. There are good reasons for being constant. Visual judgment during the approach is difficult for the novice to master, and its parameters differ with each type of momentum RW approach. It introduces too many perception variables into a situation that is confused enough.

Experienced RW'ers often vary their approach considerably, depending on exit order or the timing of the exit, but the novice will do well to find an approach "groove" and stick to it while learning.

It is especially important to keep your body in a constant half-flared coasting configuration on final approach. Set up as far out as you can and then coast "down the pipe" to the star, making smooth corrections all the way. Keep your eyes on the target wrists. Be aware of what your legs are doing. Fly straight into the star because last second turns are very hard to gauge.

Final Approach Angle

The experienced relative worker sees the ground below him as a huge bowl, the brim being the horizon. When a star or other RW formation is in the distance it is difficult to tell how far away it is except by its size. What serves the RW'er best is to think: "This star is 45° below me." If this angle decreases drastically you are going to be low on your final approach unless you are already close. If this angle increases, you are going to be too high. This is another judgment to be considered when setting up your final approach.

As you come in on final approach, things start to happen fairly fast. Even if you are right in the groove for a good, solid docking, you will probably encounter some star movement requiring constant adjustments. Make them fast. It is much easier to make corrections 10-20 ft. away from the star rather than close in.

How can you judge if you're going to make it? One clue is an old accuracy trick. Check the apparent motion of your target—wrists. Two things will be happening at once. First, the star is growing rapidly in apparent size because you are approaching it. At the same time, all of the star will show some motion as it grows.

Keep your eyes on wrists and remember this: if your target wrists move downward, however slightly, you are going to overshoot; if the wrists move upward you are about to undershoot. You will easily contact the objects that remain stationary in your field of vision. It's just like shooting accuracy—with the disc moving in three dimensions!

Borrow another accuracy technique to make sure you'll make it. Set up your approach so that you know you can reach the far side of the star in your trajectory. You can always use more brakes but you can't get more drive as easily if you need it.

Another good key is the way things look when everything is going well. Next time you are in a star, check out how the people across the star from you appear. Set this in your mind. They will look the same way, i.e. have the same perspective, every time. When you're about to dock and enter, check what you see; if it doesn't look right, it probably is not right.

Chapter VI
Docking & Flying the Star

The whole symphony of freefall relative work is shaped toward the crescendo of entry into the formation, or docking. This instant of contact with your brother and sister flyers must be precisely executed. In other maneuvers a relative worker can continually correct his mistakes as they become apparent to him. The final approach, for example, is usually a series of small corrections. At the moment of contact with the star, however, any error becomes alarmingly apparent to everyone involved. To avoid mistakes, embarrassment and small stars, you should know how to dock and enter.

The first bit of confusion arises outside the star—what is the correct speed for closing? If you go in too slowly you will bounce off the air (burble) around the star and won't be able to get in. If you go a little too fast you will set the star into a wobbly mess or even tear it to pieces.

If you bobble or shake up the star your sloppiness gives your ego a beating. If you tear up a star, you suffer doubly. For one thing, you know you've messed up and you feel badly about it. You've also messed up the jump for the other jumpers and they usually feel compelled to give you a verbal lashing. As a result you're even more tense the next time, and since tenseness makes for bad RW it's then easy to do worse. The cycle repeats itself on the next jump and it will seem as if the sun has stopped shining for you.

On the other hand, a timid docking is no better. You wash around in the slot and end up reaching, floating and bouncing off people.

For the beginner it is no simple task to fly and dock when going very slowly. It requires visual judgment that comes only with practice. The star's movements seem magnified. Also, a slow approach and entry usually means you're using a lot of body surface to generate speed. On touching the star, this large surface exposure makes you float in the slot. You can't seem to keep your ass down and you thrash around most unprofessionally. You're tense and it shows as you flap like a dishtowel drying on a clothesline.

Relax. Do relative work with the star. Let your hips, legs and feet go limp; this will get your ass down. Loosen your pectoral muscles and allow your chest to settle down between your shoulders and arms. Then shake and break to enter.

Another cause of poor docking is the novice's delayed reaction to the changing situation. He fumbles at flying when he should be relaxing to integrate himself with the movements of the star. In RW movies, a bad docking looks comic. In *your* RW, it causes small stars and unfriendly talk.

Try approaching the star in a normal glide and level out just outside the star so that you are shooting along dead level with a bit of excess speed. As you enter the slot your level approach will not allow the star to shift under you since you'd bump off their sides first. Keep your hands and arms bent in front of you, fingers ready to grasp. Use your shoulders and legs and head and ass to help you fly your entire body.

Remember that you must do bank turns or slide to effect a change in direction if you find the star, or yourself, orbiting.

Let your speed carry you onto wrists. Do not reach. If you are going to hit solidly, cushion your entry by docking with your forearms, elbows and hands to distribute the shock and avoid bending the star inward.

Analysis of RW photos and movies shows that most good dockings are made with knees down. The final approach may be from any angle, but on contact with the star, docking, the knees are down.

The reason for this is simple. When you break wrists, you naturally spread out your arms. This is a flared position and you'll "float." If your body is level or a little ass-high, this slight float will wash you up in the slot. If you tense up at this critical moment, you can flip over the star. If you are slow in relaxing into the slot, you will be sloppy. Get your knees down to avoid all that.

Elements of Docking

1. Make a level final approach (the last five to ten feet.)
2. Do not reach.
3. Take up docking shock with your forearms.
4. Preliminarily grab wrists.
5. Settle into the slot, get your ass down, fly with the star.
6. Finalize your grip.
7. Shake and break to enter the star.
8. Smile. (Ear to ear.)

Do each step in order. Don't try to skip a step. Later your entry will smooth out and seem to be a single, nearly instantaneous motion. But for the time being, learn the basics and apply them.

Using Depth Perception

Some of the judgment you will use in docking maneuvers is based on depth perception. Depth perception results from our having two eyes set apart in our head. This stereo vision provides a perception of distance.

Pure depth perception works only at about 100 feet or closer. But you also use indirect depth perception, such as size of objects, shape, perspective, etc. to determine distances. These indirect means of determining distance can be learned.

To understand how you visually judge your altitude, try jumping in the east and then move to the desert. It's easy to misjudge your altitude if you set up a landing over shrubs that you thought were really trees. It is well documented that water presents even greater problems.

Thus you have both direct and indirect clues with which to judge depth and, indirectly, speed (rate of depth change). Since these indicators require experience to recognize, they must be practiced, even by people who have perfect vision.

The fact that even one-eyed RW'ers can dock and enter demonstrates that judgment of closeness in docking can be broken down into learnable detail. It becomes easy if you know what to look for.

How to Judge a Docking

As you approach the star, keep your vision relaxed and your peripheral vision tuned in. Take in the whole star and the people entering it. Keep moving. Notice their relative size and perspective—their angle to you. Each relative worker in your visual picture can appear in a particular perspective only from a certain height. A single glance tells you how high you are above the formation.

Try it—look at RW photos—you can judge the photographer's height and angle fairly accurately by looking at the perspective of the people in the picture.

Experienced relative workers may say "I don't use that stuff..." though they probably do but without conscious effort. But then this book is for novice RW'ers who want to become "experienced" faster than those of us who learned by experimentation. Again, it is a matter of knowing what to look for; once you recognize it, it becomes nearly reflexive and you will cease having to consciously watch for it.

As you make your final approach, watch perspective indicators of whether you are rising or sinking on the star. The slightest rise will warn you that your relative fall is too slow. You may be too "big," or tense and stiff. In that case, relax into the RW Stable position and sink back to the proper level.

The slightest sink will warn you that your relative fall is too fast—too "heavy," or too tight. Spread out a bit. If your speed slackens, induce a glide into your spreadout position.

Your indicator of rise and sink—a sensitive indicator—is the perspective of the star before you. How, then, do you gauge docking, closing speed and such? You usually tend to try to watch everything at the same time: height, speed, body attitude and star movement. This is interesting but useless.

The thing to watch while docking is the intended docking spot—wrists—and secondly, the people around your target and the perspective in which they appear.

Momentum

You need momentum while docking—excess speed which you dissipate till you're going only a bit too fast, say 10 per cent, just before you reach wrists. Use the cushioned entry described on page 58.

Perhaps the star will move and you'll need this extra measure of speed to follow your slot and dock. Speed/momentum on docking helps in two ways. It gives you quick, positive control in all respects, and it docks you firmly, allowing your ass and center of gravity to sink below the level of your arms before you enter.

Docking Maneuvers

Your contribution toward building the RW formation starts when you first touch it. Any flying that you do outside and around the star which unfairly impedes others is not acceptable.

All too often novices equate touching the formation with nearly being "in." Poppycock! Making contact with the star means nothing unless you can fly in close formation with it and not disturb its flying.

The structural integrity of the formation must always out-rank your ego-centered desire to be "in." That is why, as mentioned already, the very first thing you must do when you get close to wrists is to settle in with the group before you make contact. Get your ass down, relax your legs, don't kick, un-bow and relax your shoulders, verify your grip. Then you will feel that you are part of the star. Only then should you shake and break to enter.

After 50 or so stars this whole process will take only part of a second. But until you get that experience, be sure to settle, dock and relax before you break. Otherwise you may take the star out or wash it about so badly that it either self-destructs or becomes so unstable no one else can safely enter. Contrarily, if you make contact and can't get settled into the slot, you can usually let go and flare back out for a better re-docking.

If you tend to sink in your slot after docking, correct your position of relative fall to maintain altitude and stay level with your side of the formation. If a full flare (legs outstretched, spread apart) with reverse arch won't do the trick, then you aren't doing it properly (ask an experienced relative worker), or you need a bigger jumpsuit.

The most common docking problem novice RW'ers encounter is floating in the slot. All too frequently the inexperienced RW'er will enter the slot a bit too slow and the "burble" will stop him just short of wrists. Frantically he reaches and makes "contact." But the act of reaching increases his effective size which decreases his rate of fall so that he begins to float. More frantically he tightens his grip and holds on to ride it out, usually straightening his legs in the effort. This causes increased floating which pulls his side of the formation up and pushes it toward the center.

As his ass and legs rise higher he holds on tighter, bowing his shoulders to get a "better" grip. This causes still more floating and he flips through the center or falls on someone's back. Or someone else may try to enter and the wobbly star collapses. Or tension on the star gets so bad that someone else, usually on the other side of the star, drops a grip. In any event a mess always results and everyone falls into the tunnel of a funnel.

Let's replay that mess and assume our nervous novice can follow advice. First, when he finds his approach speed to be too slow to get him onto wrists, he should flare into

Going too slowly to
penetrate the "burble",
'A' reaches to make contact.

Reaching causes him to float up.
Reaching down in panic now,
he floats even more.

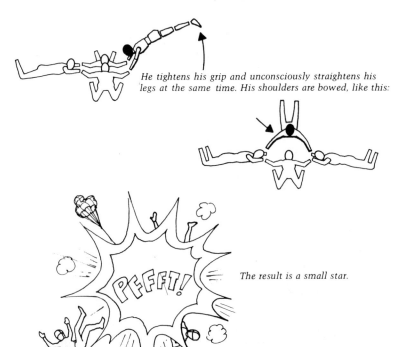

He tightens his grip and unconsciously straightens his
legs at the same time. His shoulders are bowed, like this:

The result is a small star.

Fig. 25. Docking: The Wrong Way.

recovery and fly backwards up and out of the slot, then dipping forward to gain momentum for a proper redocking.

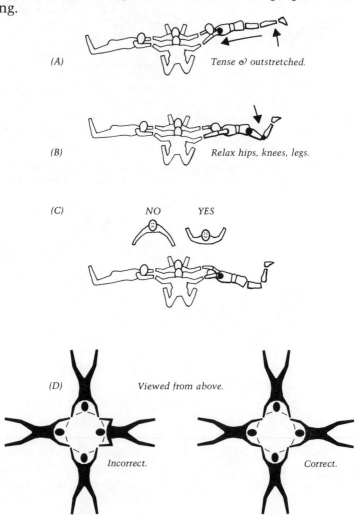

Fig. 26. Docking: The Right Way.

If he is stiff with outstretched legs, bowed arms, tense body and confused mind, (Fig. 26-A) he should consciously calm his mind as he wills his legs, knees and hips to relax, letting the wind blow them up out of the way (Fig. 26-B). He should then relax his shoulders, letting his head and chest sink lower than his arms (Fig. 26-C). If he finds he is still floating he should push his head and body away from the center toward the outside of the ring of hands. This will pivot his body downward (Fig. 26-D).

He'll be stable enough to enter after any one of these actions although all these maneuvers may need to be called into play. If his side of the star tends to push in toward the center, making the circle an oval, he should throw his head back, too.

In a good entry the axis of the body intersects the center of the star, perpendicular to a tangent line drawn across wrists. In other words, be sure you are headed straight into the slot. All too often, when entering a turning star, a novice will simply turn his head and change only his heading to follow the slot around, while his body continues in the original direction. These types of entries are not often successful. Remember, RW turns must accomplish a change in direction of movement, not just a change of heading alone. This is where a bank turn is necessary.

Grips

When the time comes to take a grip, try to be precise in your hand placement. Aim for wrists. If your hands are suited to it and the wrist you grasp is not too large, wrist grips are fine. A jumpsuit grip is preferred for small hands. Belled jumpsuits offer handy gripping surfaces. When you make a jumpsuit grip, reach over the wrist area to grab the loose fabric on the inside surface. For security and added strength, twist the material in your hands to "lock in."

Getting a good, firm grip is important, but novices frequently concentrate so much on the grip they stiffen and forget to fly. Don't forget to fly your body and use your mind while your hands are occupied with getting a good grip.

If you lose grips often you should be doing hand-strengthening exercises. Get a couple of sponge rubber balls. Have one at home and keep one in your car. Squeeze 'em to strengthen fingers and hands.

Flying the Star

After you've successfully entered, you immediately start a new phase of relative work flying—contact RW, or flying the star. Start out with a good grip.

When you're settled be sure your elbows are at a 90° angle and that your side of the star is level with the opposite side. Your job is to keep your arms at this angle and the star round and level to make it easy for others to enter.

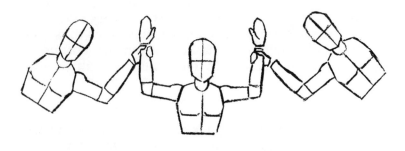

Fig. 27. Maintain 90° arm angle to fly the star.

Holding your arms at 90° reduces the possibility of someone losing a grip. Try this on the ground. Have a friend hold his arm at 90° while you simulate an entry. Now put tension on the grip—it's easy to hold on. If he straightens his arm, however, it becomes very hard to hold on. Be sure your arms are at 90° as you fly the star.

The main trick to flying the star is to relax. Everything you do in the star is also being done by the people beside you, and then must be countered by those across the star, then re-countered by you. If everyone relaxes, very slow, smooth, relaxed corrections will keep the star perfect. Learn to fly *with* the star—it's a big part of RW. If the star isn't being flown well, those outside it will have difficult entries, making it an even worse flying star.

On stars larger than a three-man, never take a base down to "help out" someone who has gone below. This nearly always hurts the final star much more than it helps because you will be making it harder for those who have already set up their final approach by changing the position of the star.

While inside the star your job is to fly the star to make it as easy as possible for **everyone** else on the load to get in. The guy who missed will have to take care of himself; he'll get there or learn something about approaches and reverse arch for his next jump. In the meantime the star will have a chance to build to its maximum size with maximum enjoyment for all (except you-know-who).

If everyone flying a star bends his knees and sits up to increase tension on the star, the star will be stronger and better able to withstand hard-hitting entries. However, this should be done only for stars of ten people or less because it puts increased tension on grips. Larger stars should be flown in "neutral."

Don't try to fly the whole star by yourself. Relative work is the sharing of an experience which requires synchronized movement among a lot of people. **Relax, don't overfly, pay attention, feel the vibes, dig it.**

Exit from a C-130.   *Carl Boenish.*

Chapter VII
Exits from Large Aircraft

Exit … leave the plane … bombout … none of these words convey the energy and coordinated scrambling of the sprinting pell-mell rush through the door of a twin-engine aircraft on a large-star jump.

You know what I mean if you've ever felt the power and emotion of a competition exit. It's an awesome attempt to have the shortest distance possible between the front man and the last man in the lineup with the most miniscule amount of time elapsing between the first and the last man leaving the door.

The exit is beyond question the most important part of a speed star. The exit has more effect on your recorded star time in competition than any other element of the jump. Most championship 10-man teams agree that fully 70-80 per cent of your recorded time on a jump is directly related to your exit time.

In speed stars forget notions about good airwork being key. Remember that all good speed-star teams do their airwork well. The only place there's room to reduce speed-star times when everyone is flying at peak is to speed up the exit. I repeat, the exit is the most important part of a jump for time.

The minutest gap somewhere in the exit doubles itself with each person behind it. Thus even a fraction of a second reduction in exit time will give you stars that are several seconds faster.

The overwhelming importance of exits means you must concentrate four times as hard on them. Several practice exits should be made before **every** load until the exit and lineup "feel" right to everyone. When it is too windy to jump, many teams practice exits with their gear on. If you have a team member who won't or can't get enthusiastic about fast exits and the practice of them, either help him to improve or remove him from the team. It *is* that important if the team is serious about competition. If your group can't manage perfect teamwork on the exit, you won't be able to make really fast speed stars.

Theory of a Fast Exit

The ideal exit has three important characteristics:

1) The *shortest amount of distance possible* between the first man and the last man in the lineup.
2) On exit, this distance between the first and the last man does not increase.
3) Even after exiting, the base endeavors to stay as close to the last man as possible.

Championship teams take full advantage of the existing rules on exiting. Team members position themselves like pieces of a jigsaw puzzle...contorting, bending, stooping, squatting, perching or whatevering to make the distance between the first and last man as short as possible. If you're comfortable in the lineup you are probably slow. Your position may be so bizarre the only thing that gets you out the door is the push of those behind you.

There's a big difference between what constitutes the best exit for you personally and what gives the entire team the best or fastest exit. It's the team effort that counts and if you are uncomfortable, that's just too bad. Your job as a team member is to make a superhuman effort to get the last man out FAST.

Of course small, low-profile gear helps to tighten up an exit. It can make a real difference when team scores get within tenths of seconds of each other.

After your group has figured out and practiced the exit lineup both with and without gear, you must convert this static exit position into a dynamic, electric, simultaneous launch of the entire team into space. A coordinated launch is effected by a proper verbal countdown.

The countdown leader must have perfect, constant cadence. His rhythm mustn't vary. He starts the count and conducts it like a choirmaster. Everyone counts LOUD! Everyone sways together with each beat. On "GO!!" everybody moves. You don't wait for the guy in front of you to move, you move NOW!

Even on fun "garbage" or pick-up loads, it's extremely worthwhile to run through a couple of practice exits. There may be some sky-god who feels he doesn't need the practice, but remind him that the jump is costing *everyone* money and that you need his cooperation and expert guidance on a couple of practice exits. (You smooth talker, you!)

When jumping a small-door aircraft, *stay low* as you dash for the door so you won't have to bend when you reach it. Take short, quick shuffling duck-walk steps. Keep your hands and body on the man in front of you. Dive *before* you get to the door.

If you do it right, you'll find your face touching the backs of the legs of the man in front of you. If you're any further away than that, then you're just not exiting properly. Some people like to hold onto diagonal or leg straps of the person in front of them to ensure there will be no gap as they leave together. Don't worry about causing him or her to go unstable...it can't possibly happen with a forceful enough exit. But be very careful not to push that individual *into* the door frame if you are lunging forward from behind him at an angle.

Exit and the Relative Wind

On exit, your aircraft will have an indicated airspeed of between 80 and 120 miles per hour. When you leave the door, it is this aircraft-generated wind, not the wind produced by your downward fall, on which you do your first few seconds of sub-terminal RW. It's like traveling down the highway in an automobile and holding your arm out the window. You'll feel a strong wind coming from the direction in which the car is traveling—this is the Relative Wind.

Remember this Relative Wind on every exit; use it to your advantage. Let it help you fly toward the star.

How you use the Relative Wind will depend on when you exit the aircraft. If you exit first or second, as part of the base, you must glide or body-surf along with it. You want to keep traveling with the airplane so that when the last men exit, they don't have too far to go to reach you.

If you exit first as a floater, again you must body-surf along with the airplane, tracking on the Relative Wind, so you can catch up with the base-pin men following you.

If you exit in the last half of the load you must execute a strong full flare against the Relative Wind so that you are not carried along with the airplane. You are trying to slow down as quickly as possible so you can begin to work on the star which is behind the aircraft.

If you simply exited and tracked for the star right away, you would actually move away from it until your aircraft-generated speed dissipated itself. Only after that would your track begin to take effect and you would start to move toward the star.

If you can exit with a brief full flare against the Relative Wind of exit, you will pick up 50 to 75 feet toward the star versus a jumper who only exits and waits for his track to take effect.

Depending on the speed of the exit and type of aircraft, the third and fourth men must stay high above the base-pin and thus be able to compensate for any turns, shifts or bobbles they may make. Whether they must flare or surf depends on what happens to the base and how fast the pin is made.

Practical Application of Exit Technique

Do each step of the exit in proper order. Don't anticipate the next step; concentrate instead on doing each segment to the best of your ability.

First, get into position and visually check that you're properly set to go. Second, calm and clear your mind for the exit. Take a deep breath and exhale slowly; feel your energy build. On the countdown, count out loud! Concentrate one-pointedly upon the rhythm, cadence and energy buildup of the countdown.

Third, on "GO!!!" get your body moving immediately, releasing energy into a controlled plunge down the
hall. Stay low and do not make unnecessary movements.
Keep your hands and body on the man in front of you,
move with him as a unit. Everyone in the line should
move as a chorus line of dancers, or a football lineup.

Fourth, launch yourself toward the door and dive out.
Fifth, find the Relative Wind of exit and use it properly.
Sixth, start moving into your descent-dive or whatever
approach you are using.

But do each of these things separately and perfectly. It
will seem disjointed at first, but practice will smooth it
out after several jumps. Speed comes only with proper
practice and not from simply trying harder. Exit skill goes
hand in hand with ability, and ability comes with practice
and concentration on each part of the exit.

8-Donut Flake.   *Rande Deluca.*

Chapter VIII
Equipment for Relative Work

 Back when I was jumping in Texas, more than 20 years ago, my favorite jump-wear was a skin-tight pair of coveralls. I liked 'em to fit tight 'cause they looked better—more tailored, y'know. On really hot days I usually opted for cut-off blue jeans, a T-shirt and cowboy boots.

My reserve was mounted real high 'cause that's where the U.S. Army Parachute Team wore theirs. My surplus B-4 harness and backpack were adjusted to their largest size because that's where they eventually slipped anyway. Mainly I didn't care how anything fit. Relative work was called "fun jumping" then, and all my group did was "fun jump."

My rig fit so loosely it would slip off my shoulders and lay around me in a pile as the Cessna 195 climbed to altitude. So tight was the tailoring on my jumpsuit that I commonly flew in a full spread. I thought I was hot stuff. I could exit fifth at 7200 ft. and get in third by 1500 ft. That was considered to be good.

What took me so long to get in, besides the fact that *nobody* could do RW then (except a handful of guys in California), was a lot more than just my poor technique. About seven years later part of the reason finally sunk in... *Your parachute gear is part of the airplane that is your body*!

Fantastic! Gear *does* make a difference! If you arrange your jumpsuit and equipment in an optimum configuration, you can be more effective and efficient at relative work. I'd like to share my thoughts on equipment for RW with you.

General Notes on Equipment

First, some overall observations on the elements of gear:

Jumpsuit...made to measure for you; fits well with underarm "wing" area and thighs balanced so that your upper and lower body can fly on the same plane. Clearly the jumpsuit is the most important part of the relative worker's equipment. Today's jumpsuit has evolved into a "flightsuit." Extra material in the arm, leg and wing area provides control surfaces for flight.

Proper measurement is a must for good fit. Your mass to size ratio should be considered when making your order. A 150 lb. six-footer would want a different amount of material in his jumpsuit than a 200-lb.'er of the same height.

Putting an oversized jumpsuit on an inexperienced relative worker is foolish. Every movement tends to be exaggerated, and floating becomes a considerable problem for many. An exception, of course, is the fireplug... extra heavy types who tend to go below any RW group, even in a full spread. These flying bowling balls need a big jumpsuit.

Rig...snug-fitting harness system that is light and has a small profile. Lightweight gear makes freefall flight easier.

Main canopy...one that lets you down easy and is light and maneuverable; packs up small.

Boots/Shoes . . . tennis or running shoes, Indian moccasins (wrap-type) or other lightweight footwear that helps your feet to feel the air. Your feet are just as important as your hands in relative work.

Gloves. . . thin, or none. Again, the goal is to be able to feel the relative wind and use it effectively. In the winter, use good quality ski gloves with lots of "feel." Water ski gloves have a good gripping surface—wear glove liners underneath for warmth.

Helmet . . . one that doesn't get in the way. Your head is a sensitive judge of the relative wind. Wear the lightest helmet you can find that provides the amount of head protection you can be comfortable with. Heavy helmets designed for auto racing and motorcycling are an unnecessary burden to the experienced relative worker. There are many suitable models of hockey helmets available.

Goggles . . . some that allow good vision. Portias, jockey goggles and "boogie" glasses are okay. People who wear eyeglasses find that they can be strapped on and serve as fairly good goggles—so do wraparound sunglasses.

Other. . . it is helpful if someone on the load wears an altimeter. . . and uses it.

Choosing Gear. . . Where To Start

Maybe you're a beginner, or are considered unskilled. To get better, start with your rig: the harness/container system.

Buying a rig that fits your particular needs requires some thought. How do you fall?. . .fast?. . .slow? In what position are your arms and legs when you close on the formation? Do you have to tuck up. . .or spread out. . .a lot? Do you find yourself flying with your arms outstretched above your head? Do you always float on the formation, or are you usually low in it? Think about it! Ask people.

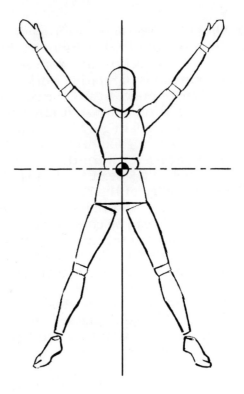

Fig. 28. Center of Gravity.

*Your center of gravity is just below your navel, in a line intersecting
your hip bones. Lay across a bar and stiffen into a full spread to find
it. When you fly, fly with your stomach, not your head or "the seat of
your pants."*

Once you get answers to these questions, think
about them in relation to the center of gravity of your
body. Roughly calculate how your rig may adversely
affect your relative work. In a "normal" flight position
you should be relaxed and RW stable. You should not
have to keep your arms outstretched, or your legs
tucked in, or anything else strange.

The brand of rig you choose isn't really critical. It doesn't matter who made the gear you have. It's like tennis or skiing. The racquet or skis and boots you feel comfortable and confident with are largely a matter of preference. Whatever you get, make sure it's small and lightweight. Your gear should be as light as that flown by others with whom you are flying.

Surviving the Move to New Gear

If you are jumping conventional gear with the reserve on the front, or an older tandem system, your first big move toward becoming a skygod will likely be the purchase of a new-era tandem system. Often you'll buy the fanciest, most advanced system because you plan to jump it for a long time.

If you can handle yourself well in freefall, you will likely do okay with your new gear if you pay attention to a few basics.

Handling yourself in freefall doesn't mean to be "good" at RW. It means that you can stay stable, or not worry about being unstable. Try this . . . put your right hand on your right hip in freefall for 3-5 seconds. Can you handle it? Did you stay stable? Do you realize that it is okay to pull unstable? When you have a choice of either pulling or regaining stability, the wise jumper will pull. It is considered very poor form to go in without pulling; you get zero points for stability if you fail to pull.

Can you walk and chew gum at the same time? In other words, can you contemplate the possible new location of your ripcord whilst counting off the passing time whilst watching others track to pull when you are already low to start with?

Are you familiar with your new rig? Did you wear it around the house for awhile on several days last week? Did you spend time over several days touching the important parts while you were wearing the rig?

Make a familiarization jump by yourself. Plan to pull at 3000 ft. on at least a 30-second delay. A jump spent increasing your survival potential is *never* a wasted jump.

Don't rush your first pack job on the new rig. Have several competent people verify that your assembly of the pack job will likely work. It is far better to catch a silly packing/assembly error on the ground than to have to dump your reserve on your first jump on the rig.

Here is the procedure I think you should consider when moving on to advanced gear. By paying attention to these things, you will improve your survival potential. And since survival is the only condition that allows you to make more high-energy, fun-filled skydives, it's worth the time and effort.

1. Be current. Don't make your first jump in many weeks on borrowed or new gear without a good ground-practice session with it.
2. Put the new rig on over your jumpsuit, just like you plan to jump it. Can you see the ripcords? Can you find them by feel? Does the ripcord feel like part of your harness or jumpsuit so that you might confuse them in freefall?
3. Practice standing or laying down . . . imagine you are in freefall. Go through the motions of pulling your main. Any problems there? Practice pulling your cutaway and then your reserve. Did you use the same hand? If so, can you pull your reserve with the cutaway handle in your hand too?
4. Did you remember to look down for canopies below you before cutting away?
5. Will you actually remember to count? Time can seem to compress or expand in a tense situation. There is no way that you can keep track of altitude without counting. Nearly getting your reserve out before impact is not good enough. Count.
6. Do you plan to tug on the risers to clear the malfunction? This has worked sometimes

for some people. Many others have died looking up and trying to sort out a mess as they thunder into the dirt. Don't play with it; get rid of it.

7. How will you handle a pilot chute in tow? How will you pack to ensure you will not experience pilot-chute-in-tow? What sort of pin check will you need with your new rig?

8. What will you do if the hand-deployed pilot chute wraps around your hand, arm, neck or foot?

9. How should you get your hand-deploy off of your burble? If you have to pull your reserve for what feels like a total (pack closure), how do you know it is not a pilot chute in tow? How do you know that it is not just hesitating in your burble, ready to leave and entangle with your reserve?

10. What is your procedure when you can't find your main ripcord handle? How long do you plan to look for it? How do you know when it is time to give up and use your reserve?

11. What will you do if someone pulls right under you?

12. If you get involved in a canopy entanglement with someone else, what will you do?

13. Let's say you were doing RW with some friends and everybody forgot the altitude until ground rush started getting fierce. What will you do?

Pull-out from a 9-Diamond.   Ray Cottingham.

Chapter IX
Assigned Slots: Pattern Flying and the Quadrant System

Being at a specific place within a limited amount of time is an integral part of all relative work. When there are several people involved and available time is at a premium, traffic becomes a problem. If ten people exit and track for the same contact point on the star, the result is called "chaotic" and the formation usually ends in a funnel.

It's common, even now, to see some star loads, particularly large-star attempts, where 90 per cent of the people are attempting to enter 30 per cent of available slots—those that are on the closest side of the star. That one side loads up and builds too fast, making the star impossible to fly. In this case, even those few who may have flown around to the back side of the star are hampered, because the mob on the other side is usually pushing, floating or otherwise messing up the star so that it is anything but stable.

A star which is building too fast on one side will usually begin to slide across the sky at alarming speed. Sometimes it moves so fast it "eats" unwary would-be entrants. This gives rise to the old saw, "It slid right under me, honest!"...an excuse that is usually indigestible to all of those on the crowded side who were "waiting their turn to enter."

This traffic jamming also puts a lot of strain on the star, frequently resulting in a dropped grip.

Once upon a time, someone plucked their head out of the nether region and correctly surmised that if the star were imagined to be a clock face, then each flyer could be assigned a particular slot...say, two o'clock, or four o'clock, six, nine, etc. Or the star could be divided into quadrants like a compass, and everyone would have their specific quadrant, say, "northwest."

This did help to eliminate traffic but it created another problem...befuddlement. Many people are lousy at telling left from right, or can't remember where 12 o'clock is in freefall.

Another system, the people and places method, has also been tried. In this system you enter between two pre-assigned people. The word "usually" is key here, because if the star turns or one of the people you're to enter on blows it, you have to improvise.

The method that seems to work best is the fastest and the simplest. It's a combination of assigned slot flying and the quadrant system.

To avoid confusion, any part of the star which is closest to the exit door of the airplane is appropriately called THE *NEAR* SIDE of the star. The other side of the star, the one farthest from the door, is called THE *FAR* SIDE of the star. These near and far sides are further divided into left and right. (If you get confused on left vs. right, just remember that your right hand usually pulls the ripcord; stick the left one in your ear, if you like, unless you're left-handed.)

Now, no matter how the star may turn, you maintain your assigned quadrant and fly the same pattern. For example, if your slot is in the LEFT-NEAR quadrant, you will always exit the plane and fly slightly left and then straight into the left hand part of the near side of the star. If the star should turn, you disregard the turning and still fly the same pattern. The people you enter between may change, but where you enter the star in relation to the airplane is constant. (See Figure 29.)

In assigning slots, take into consideration how each person flies. Some people are much faster using a straight-in approach. They will work best on the near side of the star. Other people like to use a "catch up turn" or back-door entry. They should go to the far side.

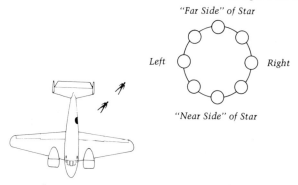

Fig. 29. Quadrant System.

Importantly, you should probably have the 9th and 10th men fly to the near side for speed stars since it affords them a direct line, straight-in shot for the fastest time. In this case, 7th and 8th will go to the far side (left and right). Since this is a longer flying distance, you might consider putting your fastest people here.

Two example exit orders might be: first, an ordinary lineup.

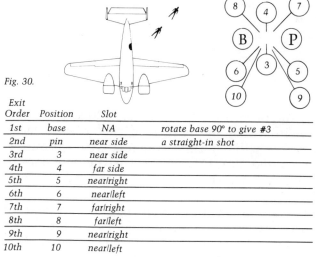

Fig. 30.

Exit Order	Position	Slot	
1st	base	NA	rotate base 90° to give #3
2nd	pin	near side	a straight-in shot
3rd	3	near side	
4th	4	far side	
5th	5	near/right	
6th	6	near/left	
7th	7	far/right	
8th	8	far/left	
9th	9	near/right	
10th	10	near/left	

Or, if you use floaters:

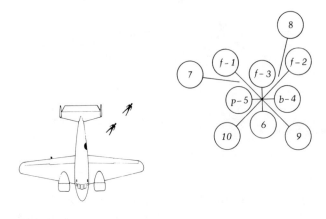

Fig. 31.

Exit Order	Position	Slot	
1st	floater-1	far/left	
2nd	floater-2	far/right	
3rd	floater-3	far	
4th	base	far	
5th	pin	near	
6th	#3	near	
7th	#4	far/left	NOTE: *FLOATERS:*
8th	#5	far right	*don't rush it,*
9th	#6	near/right	*let #3 stable out*
10th	#7	near/left	*the base.*

It is important to note in Figures 30 and 31 that the direction in which the base turns in order to face the oncoming pin will determine the relative positions of the base-pin combo. But, *whichever* way the base does turn, the others still fly their quadrants and patterns as assigned.

Most base-men turn to their right on exiting, though some turn to their left. Turning right is said to be more natural and easier. Turning left is said to be harder but keeps the base-pin closer to the airplane.

Chapter X
Precision Freefall Team
Relative Work Maneuvers
and Sequential Plays

 The visual exultation of seeing fine precision relative work flying on film is surpassed only by the joy of being part of the jump yourself. With precise control you fly an individual RW dance that intertwines and connects with others in geometric shapes, and then, perhaps, sequences into yet another maneuver. It fills your heart and soul with exhilaration. It's legal!

Fantastic figures in billowy rainbows of colored gear swoop like a Phoenix on the living pattern as it builds in a slow motion, coordinated dance on the uprushing air. Each flyer seems to be performing his own ballet in beautiful unity with the others.

Perhaps you dress in stunning brilliances of color which your freefall brothers can add to the technicolorful, three-dimensional movie they are watching, as their imaginations collectively ebb and flow into the completed maneuver.

Think of the blinding blue of two miles high, and the duller patchwork of earth that frames the flying pattern. Only an occasional flashing cloud notices the masterpiece till it explodes in a rocket burst ending in flowering canopies. If only film could also capture the 500,000-watt energy flow, and the thundering symphony of sound..."Roll-over, Beethoven—tell Tchaikovsky the news!"

A good fast exit and speed are required in all forms of relative work. In competition speed stars, speed and skill in the exit, descent, flare, and docking/entry maneuvers are vital. In good speed stars, all flying is classified as momentum RW. Flyers maintain the momentum of their descent/track and redirect it to enter the star, without ever stopping. In good sequential relative work, flying is classified as both momentum and non-momentum RW. Flyers maintain the momentum of the descent/track and carefully redirect it to fill their slot. Then the entire formation may transition into non-momentum RW to build a sequential maneuver(s).

Both speed-star and sequential RW require a good exit. And in both, the base is key.

While most people like any kind of RW, some people like one type better than another. Neither is superior nor inferior to the other. It depends on what you like to do. Some prefer sequential or alternate maneuver flying because it's more immediately fun than all the concentrated team jumps you have to make to be good at 10-man speed stars.

Alternate maneuvers and sequential "plays" do require more flying from all the people on the team. Everyone is assigned a particular slot and plays are run as in football. No one can be late for their slot, or get low, because there are other people waiting for him to fill his position before they can take theirs. Diagrams of the plays are usually required, often filed in a team's "playbook."

Since the plays themselves are hard to visualize, even on paper, you have to do a lot of ground practice for successful sequential RW. When you begin, start small (four to six people) and build up. A lot of the maneuvers that seem complex are simply constructed from smaller segments. Practice these four to six-person segments to learn how to "helicopter," to fly backwards, and to switch grips. Grip switching gives symmetry to the sequence from maneuver to maneuver.

The "switch signal" system is key. The last man in shakes his grip and it is telegraphed around the pattern. The runners drop their grips and helicopter to the next contact area, while grips are switched throughout the pattern until the next maneuver is completed.

You'll find that loads of either four, ten, 16 or 20 are best for symmetrical plays and sequential maneuvers.

As the first maneuver in a sequential RW skydive builds, precision is critical. You must dock at your assigned position so as to have no effect on the building maneuver's stability. Others wait to enter, or await your entry, to settle in and help fly the pattern to completion.

When you're in a maneuver like a French Connection, a Wedge or a Tripod, you may be somewhat visually isolated from the center of the figure. Because of this, you must pay particular attention to your relative flying so that your position and flying attitude do not give unwanted movement to the whole pattern. Watch the ground. Watch the other flyers in the pattern. Feel your attitude.

When you get the switch signal, act immediately. In unison with the others, fly to your next contact area. Fast non-momentum RW requires full use of your body. Get into it. Gain a bit of altitude while you hand-track. Drop/glide/helicopter into your next slot...you may even be called on to fly backwards! Fly it!

Never expect the pattern to absorb any excess speed you have. Docking shock will snap a ripple through it that may amplify into a wave of self-destruction. Be precise. Put your body where it is supposed to be. Make a no-wrinkle entry. Get a caressing but vise-like grip on your contact man's jumpsuit, or somewhere that won't impede his ability to help fly the maneuver.

If you're on the outer ends, make sure you don't unconsciously turn the maneuver either clockwise or counter-clockwise. Don't float or sink. Be aware. If you fly at the point, or front, be very careful. Have a good sense for where *straight down* is, and use it.

On break-up, turn away from the maneuver and max-track away from its imagined center before you wave off to pull.

The word "play" used in planning alternate maneuver and sequential skydives comes from "football play." Similarities between the two plays are very direct.

In any professional football play, each man on the team has a particular assignment, and the play is not successful unless every man does his assignment well. The timing, symmetry and beautifully coordinated motion of a pro-football play can be so perfect it is awesome. In RW plays, the same is true. Everyone has a particular slot on a particular sequence and the play cannot be successfully completed unless each individual does his job well. As in football, timing and teamwork are critical.

Vertical Tri-Diamond.   *Ray Cottingham.*

Chapter XI
Sport

 "Like so much of life, football presents us with the choice of responding either with fear or with action and clarity."
—John Brodie[6]
One day, football star John Brodie got together with Michael Murphy, president of Esalen Institute, to discuss Sport. Not just the physical aspects, but the under-lying psychic elements that the uninitiated would call "occult." Their conversation, recorded in *Intellectual Digest,* reveals an aspect of Sport that is particularly applicable to skydiving. Murphy noted that some surfers, skydivers, skiers and football players talk a language that is almost mystical.

John Brodie, quarterback for the San Francisco 49'ers for more than 16 years, knows a lot about ground-team relative work. He is only one step behind Johnny Unitas for the record of yards gained passing in the NFL. He is also a championship golfer.

Michael Murphy is president and co-founder of the Esalen Institute in California, and author of *Golf in the Kingdom,* a metaphysical sports fantasy that explores what Murphy calls the "hidden side of sport."

Both men feel there is a lot to the game that has not been described by all the renowned sportswriters and football analysts. All of these spectators, knowledgeable though they be, are missing something.

Brodie says a great many football players feel the same way about the sport he does:

"There is a side to the game that really hasn't been described yet—that 'hidden' side of sport you talk about in your book, things having to do with the psychological side of the game, with what we might call 'energy flows,' and the extraordinary states of mind performing athletes sometimes get into."

Everyone injects their own reality into football—a reality that may not mesh with the actuality of the sport. Brodie's reality of the sport includes "energy flows" which he defines:

"Often, in the heat and excitement of a game, a player's perception and coordination will improve dramatically. At times, and with increasing frequency now, I experience a kind of clarity that I've never seen adequately described in a football story. Sometimes, for example, time seems to slow way down, in an uncanny way, as if everyone were moving in slow motion. It seems as if I have all the time in the world to watch the receivers run their patterns, and yet I know the defensive line is coming at me just as fast as ever. I know perfectly well how hard and fast those guys are coming and yet the whole thing seems like a movie or a dance in slow motion. It's beautiful."

What he is describing, as the Yaqui Indian sorcerer, Don Juan, points out to Carlos Castaneda in *A Yaqui Way of Knowledge*, is that you see more clearly because you are a warrior in a state which can only be defined as "non-ordinary reality."

In *Golf in the Kingdom*, Murphy discusses "energy streamers" that a golf ball rides on its way toward the hole—lines of force that seem to emanate from the golfer when he can visualize and execute his shot in a moment of high clarity.

I often experience this phenomena while skydiving. And it used to occur during fencing and racing when I engaged in those sports. My personal approach to doing relative work is predicated, in part, on this theory. Strangely, perhaps, the other part is imagined music—a classical symphony written to the roar of the airplane and the rush of the wind. Plus a beautiful vision of dancers performing an ecstatic ballet choreographed by the clouds.

All body movement, as martial arts masters state, is directed by energy flows which emanate from the area of the stomach. This idea is further substantiated by the Yogin who says the stomach is one of the principal power centers. So, you fly with your stomach as much as your head.

Yes, it sounds bizarre. But can it be learned? Can you practice and develop clarity during a relative work jump? Can you strengthen your intentions? As John Brodie says,

"Yes. Pressures that used to get me down don't affect me to the same extent now. I've learned to shed certain destructive attitudes when a game is under way. A player's effectiveness is directly related to his ability to be right there, doing that thing, in the moment. All the preparation he may have put into the game—all the game plans, analysis of movies, etc.—is no good if he can't put it into action when game time comes. He can't be worrying about the past or the future or the crowd or some other extraneous event. He must be able to respond in the here and now. This is an ability we all have potentially. I believe it is our natural state. But because most of us lose it as we grow up, we have to regain it."

Agreed, it does sound like Zen or a similar spiritual discipline. These same ideas, phrased differently, appear in the *Bhagavad-Gita,* in at least seven separate Buddhist texts (see translations by E. Y. Evans-Wentz), and also in the *Tao Te Ching* and elsewhere in Eastern religious philosophy.

As Michael Murphy said:

"It seems to me that in many ways sport is like a Western Yoga. I have heard mountain climbers, surfers, sky divers and skiers who talk a language that is almost mystical, and now I hear you talking the same way.

Brodie: Call it mystical if you like. For me it is simply one of the elementary facts of experience. Here-and-now awareness, clarity, strong intention, a person's "tone level"—these are things a lot of people who don't know anything about Yoga or mysticism talk about. The trouble is, people don't make them operative in their life as often as they could.

Murphy: But some of the things you seem to suggest, like a ball jumping over a defender's hands or time slowing down, go beyond ordinary experience. In the East, and in our Western religious traditions, there have been disciplines to develop these extraordinary powers and states of mind. But the modern Western world, for the most part, is lacking in such disciplines. They seem esoteric and alien to most of us. Maybe that is one of the reasons sportswriters and sports commentators find it difficult to comprehend the kinds of things you are talking about."

It's not surprising that people find it difficult to grasp these ideas. One of the problems is language:

"Murphy: One of the problems coaches and players have—and it's a problem all of us have in talking about these things—is that our language about unusual powers and states of mind is so limited. We don't have commonly understood words to describe "energy flows" or what you call "being clear." These expressions don't make sense to a lot of people. I think the time has come to begin creating a language and an understanding about these dimensions of life.

Brodie: Athletics could be a place where this kind of insight is developed. Sport is one of the few activities in which many Americans spend a great deal of time developing their potentialities. It influences character, I think, as much as our schools and churches do. But, even so, it falls far below what it could be. It leaves out so much. I would love to see a sports team developed with a more fulfilling purpose."

Try it. Many four-man RW teams and ten-man RW teams do have a special kind of communication in freefall. We read each other so well that we know where we need to be in a given situation. We make contact somewhere in the field of our existence, amidst all the flux and within all the sound and fury of the rushing sky. It's a highly intuitive thing. It's our thing, for there's a kind of communication, a kind of *being* if you will, that happens during an inspired jump.

And, after a jump is a lot like after a game. Brodie

mentions a statement made by Alan Page, defensive tackle for the Minnesota Vikings and NFL most valuable player for 1971. Page described his feelings of comedown after a game is over. He said it was a weird feeling adjusting back to ordinary reality, to sanity, to having to be a person again.

I know what he means. Life can be like a soap opera after a good jump. You can get into a different order of reality when you're doing RW, a non-ordinary reality that just doesn't mesh with the black-and-white-with-no-gray lines that many people use to delineate life.

When you make an RW jump, when you line up for the exit, you are tuning into the situation. You clear yourself by dropping useless emotional buildup and other distractions. Your goal is to be focused and sensitive. Don't worry about results. That's later, and later never exists.

"Relative work done with anxiety about results is far inferior to relative work done without such anxiety. In the calm of controlled abandon, seek refuge in the knowledge of the art of relative work. Those who work selfishly for results are miserable."

Adapted from the BHAGAVAD-GITA,
"Song of God"

★ ★

Brodie explains his perception of knowledge:

Brodie: I equate creativity with awareness. It's a matter of simple knowledge. The more I know, the more I can do.

Murphy: But knowing like this is more than the kind of knowing we are supposed to learn in school, more than verbal knowing or book knowing. It involves a tuning in to subtle energies and feelings and forces we can only come to through direct awareness. It involves the emotions and the spirit as well as the intellect—and the here and now, the complexities and subtleties of a given situation rather than preconceptions about it, or your rehearsals of it or what has been written in a book about it. It seems to me that this sort of knowing leads to a new kind of being.

Murphy: After hearing you talk I gather that top athletes are people who are accustomed to altering time, who are accustomed to a higher state of focus and concentration, who are accustomed to altered perceptions of many types and to going with the inner flow of things. But I don't see any of this on the sport pages. Or in the sport books you hear about, or on the radio and TV programs. Our culture seems to screen it all out, even though such experience is at the very heart of a game so many of us love.

Brodie: That's right. It's a case of experience being ahead of what we can say about it. Maybe if we could talk about it more clearly we could make it happen more. Sport is so important in creating values in America, it would be great if it could open up these inner dimensions for people. It's really what many coaches and players want to do, after all. They want sport to be more than winning at any cost, more than beating people up and making money and getting ahead over somebody else's dead body. But we have got to break out of this conspiracy to belittle sport and human nature."

And most fittingly, I think, this champion of the American sport concludes:

"It is better to improve the game, I think, than to indulge in a lot of idle criticism of it. And when you look at its history you see that it has already gone through enormous changes. It is a much different game than it was in the 1920s or 30s. It's a more complex and artistic game now, with all the offensive and defensive plays, with the game plans and the variety of skills involved. Why shouldn't the game go on changing? I see no reason why we should fix the game of football where it is, after the change it has gone through already. Why shouldn't it be a place to develop the mental and spiritual dimensions we have been talking about?"

★   ★   ★

"By letting it go it all gets done.
The world is won by those who let it go.
But when you try and try,
The world is then beyond winning."
                                    –Tao Te Ching

Double Horizontal Opposed Diamonds.

8-Bipole Flake.

8-Donut.   *Sequential series by Ray Cottingham.*

Chapter XII
Relative Work Competition and Team Organization

 Competition is an integral part of our way of life. Survival itself might be called competition with the elements. Certainly our Judeo-Christian work ethic, or the Puritan work ethic, if you will, proclaims that those who work hard will receive greater rewards than those who don't. Competition is fostered by the institutions of our society: schools, the military, the family and organizations of all types for all age groups.

Many philosophers believe that competition—the desire to excel—is one of man's basic needs. Robert Ardrey, for example, author of *African Genesis* and *The Territorial Imperative*, believes that the carving out of a personal niche, accompanied by the drive to fight for it, is more basic than any other drive, including sex.

"**Competition:** a rivalry, contest, match. ... (SYN) denotes a striving for the same object, position, prize, etc., usually in accordance with certain fixed rules." —*Webster's New World Dictionary of the American Language*[7]

Most definitions of the word "competition" center around the Ego and relate to aggrandizement of same. Many people see competition only as a quest for personal glory. The quest to "be the best," or "Number One." ... "Winning isn't everything, it's the ONLY thing" ... and "Nothing counts except first place" ... I'm sure you know many more of these brash saws.

Some relative workers pursue competition from this point of view. Others approach it a bit differently—as a chance to do the thing they really like to do with teammates with whom they feel in harmony.

[7]College Edition, 1966.

Organized RW competition provides a setting for both approaches. At the site of a meet there are many others who share your interest. It's a fun, social setting. You pay your jump money plus extra to provide toilets, trophies, extra aircraft, and profit for the hard-working organizers.

All you have to do is relax and wait for your load to be called. Then you go up and do your thing with your team. It's what you've been practicing for months. You try to do as well as you've done in practice ... as well as you've been doing over the last several jumps. You do not try to go faster. (The try-to-go-faster part was something you experimented with in practice prior to the meet.) You assume that you'll do at least as well as you usually do. Except that it's more fun because there's the electricity of a team working together, each member giving his all to win the event.

It's the same feeling you would get if you were driving a really fast car in a race, or giving your all in a high-jump event. You are a highly trained athlete, in good condition and peak form. And you're doing that which you most love to do, and that is to fly.

Types of RW Competition
There are two freefall relative work competition events recognized by the Federation Aeronautique Internationale, which makes the rules for international competition. They are the 10-man star event and the four-man sequential event. The U.S.P.A. National Parachuting Championships are held to recognize national and conference parachuting champions in four-man and ten-man team relative work performance, and "to select the top parachutists within the United States to compose a representative United States Parachute Team for participation in selected international parachuting competitions."[8]

Advantages of Being on a Team
When you jump with a team it can be a wonderful experience. You don't have to scrounge around and dredge

[8]U.S.P.A., Part 50, Competition Rules and Regulations.

up people to jump with. The team captain or manager does all the manifesting for you. You tend to get more jumps with a team because the team has collective snivel power. The manifestor knows you want to jump, that you have a load together, and that you'll get your lift off as soon as you can. That keeps the airplanes running and you jumping.

You can also learn a lot about precision RW while jumping with a team. By jumping in the same position and with the same people every time, you'll learn more about how are you flying in relation to others. They'll be a constant against which you can practice the art of flying your body. Additionally, after a while the team can accomplish esoteric RW maneuvers that probably couldn't be completed by jumpers who didn't know the steady consistency of a team and the confidence of knowing ... of being *certain* that the situation will be as planned when you arrive at your slot.

And, you get a lot of star time. Star time is that time which you spend flying *in* a star. On non-team loads you tend to spend most of the time exiting, tracking, correcting for a moving base, entering the star, and very little time flying as part of that star.

Getting star time is invaluable because it teaches you how to do contact relative work ... a very advanced type of RW in which you fly in concert with the others locked into the formation. You learn to react relative to those who are also reacting to a changing formation. The end result is a very stable formation.

A star with just a few people in it who are really heads up on star flying can make a world of difference between what gets entered in the logbook as a completed maneuver and what gets entered as an attempt. So when you're on a team, you'll be in more *completed* maneuvers. That's a nice feeling.

Then, too, there's status connected with jumping with a team. It means you're a competition RW flyer. You've shown yourself to be good enough, or at least to have the enthusiasm and stamina, to be "part of the team."

Before takeoff you don't need to drag everyone together for the load. You'll meet for ground practice before every jump. You'll practice exits with people who will really put their hearts into it because they all recognize how important the exit is to the team. Hopefully there will be no loafing, or sluggish laggards, on your team.

There's less of that old "let's just go up and see what we get" attitude. You have an assigned seat in the plane—your ticket is collected.

On jump-run the exit lineup will build professionally as the star-master spots. The exit countdown, being well rehearsed before each jump, actually helps your exit. You know the motion and sway of the lineup by heart, and you can dash to the door in cadence to get a good shotgun exit for everyone.

Outside the airplane you'll know where the star is and what your flight pattern is to be. You can then concentrate on perfecting your flying. You're familiar with the falling speed of the star so your flare-point requires less guesswork. After entry you fly in coordination with your mates. And you'll feel the electric charge of good vibes that flows through a team when it's a good jump. It's exhilarating.

At break-off time there's less worry about a midair collision or canopy pass. Back on the ground there'll be a critique of the jump that lets you know what went on and gives you an idea how and where you can improve on your next jump.

And in competition you'll have the joy and pride of pitting your hard-earned skill against others with the same interests. It can be a very rewarding experience.

How to Be a Good Team Member

The commitment required of every member of a competition relative work team is essential to the well-being and success of the team. Each member should be willing to stand before his teammates and agree to the extent of the commitment as outlined by the captain. Without full agreement among all members as to just what you are trying to do, and when and how it'll be done, you will be sowing seeds of misunderstanding that may grow into bitterness later. Don't make any assumptions. Talk it over thoroughly.

Here's a partial list of things that must be agreed to, and once agreed to, adhered to:

1. You will be available for every team practice, without exception.
2. Team practice will officially start at a certain time and day each weekend.
3. You will be present, without exception, at or before that time.
4. You will have all your gear ready to jump at that time.
5. You will be awake and alert when you appear at practice. You will announce your presence to the captain or team manager. You will be ready to put your gear on.
6. You will be a positive contributor to the team meeting.
7. You will participate in ground practice and practice exits to the best of your ability.
8. You will suit up promptly when the load is called.
9. You will have your jump ticket ready.
10. You will be considerate of your team members, and of course, you'll make your best effort on the jump.

After the jump:

1. You will attend the team meeting or pack promptly as requested.
2. If you have any angry tirades, you will keep them to yourself.
3. If you have legitimate complaints or constructive criticisms, you will pass them on quietly, tactfully and privately, if possible, to the team captain. He will handle them as he deems appropriate.
4. You will be ready for the next jump. Never keep your teammates waiting.

You should not display uncontrolled hostility or anger, because it accomplishes nothing except to put a strain on everyone. Team jumping is very trying and may be hard on your nerves. Realize this and watch for it. Remember the positive reasons you are jumping with the team.

Unjumpable weather bums out everyone. Tensions and bad feelings are harder than ever to control. If a team splits up, or has a divorce, it's often during a long spell of bad weather.

"Do Not Feed the Judges"

Judging relative work is a difficult task—and an art all its own. Judging requires a quickness of eye and extreme patience that few people possess. RW judges who are good at it will record their respective times to within three-tenths of a second of one another.

If RW competition is to continue to improve, the critical element of judging cannot be overlooked. Serious teams should develop their own training judges. This will give the team a constant source for ground timers during practice so that progress can be evaluated. Importantly, it will also provide a judge for meets who has trained as hard as the competitors themselves. The result will be better meets and more accurate judging.

The serious team should have a team fund. One of the first acquisitions should be a good quality stop watch suitable for judging. An inexpensive cassette tape recorder is also a good judge-team training aid. The recorder is used as the star forms and the judging calls made: "Exit! ... 2,3 ... 4,5 ... 6,7,8,9,10." As the tape is replayed, the team may note slow spots. The judge can re-check his time. Individual team members can keep track of their own personal progress by timing from the tape.

At meets it is important to assist the judges wherever possible. Someone should be sure they get food and drink throughout the day. The judging sites should be separated so that judges cannot hear each other's calls. Judging sites should be made as comfortable as possible, with shade from the sun.

The meet judges are trying to do their best, just as you are. How well they do depends on how well they are equipped and trained. If they're uncomfortable and hot, or can't communicate with the manifestor, meet director and aircraft easily, you can expect problems. Yes, *YOU* can expect problems. If team captains do not check out the judging setup and equipment before the first round starts, it is too late for complaints about bad judging later.

When the meet is underway, remember that you came to jump, not to hassle, complain or protest. Avoid becoming entangled in judging hassles while at a meet. If it is a so-called "fun" meet and the judging and competition is casual, it is unreasonable to complain bitterly if you get what you consider a bad call.

If you want judges who are as good at their thing as you are at yours, you must be willing to help train them and to spend more money to make their time worthwhile. This may mean higher meet entry fees to cover motel rooms, digital timers, tape recorder rental, communications equipment rental, sun shades, etc. But if you've trained hard for the meet, it should be worth it to you.

Your national parachuting organization, U.S.P.A., can often lend a hand. They have telemeters and other judging aids available for loan through Conference directors. But you must inform them, and ask for their assistance.

Team Organization

The team captain is critical to the success of the team. He must have the support of the entire team. After practice times, dates, places, and how many jumps to be made each day are agreed on by the team, the captain must make sure that these stated practice goals are accomplished. He organizes ground practice and establishes team exit order.

Since attitude and enthusiasm are critical in competition RW, the captain should be able to inspire and bring out these traits in his team as well. He is the quarterback. Team members owe him their respect and support. It's a tough job. Give your captain all the consideration you can.

The team can work together much more smoothly if it is well organized. This is not a simple task. Frequently a team will have a team manager in addition to a captain to handle these organizational problems and to help ensure that the team's time is spent effectively. Collecting money for loads, handling team communications are two important jobs that a manager can handle.

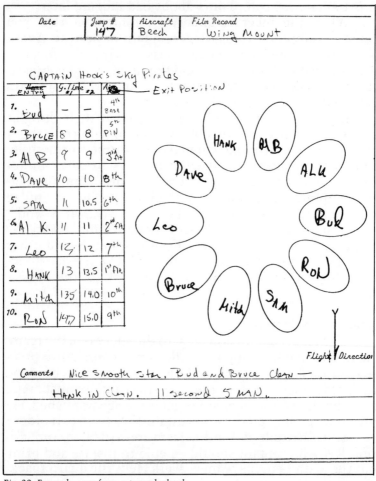

Fig. 32. Example page from a team logbook.

A team logbook is an excellent idea, too. It will show strengths and weak spots in recording progress. It can be compared with the stated team goals. It will give the team an idea of problems that may occur consistently.

As for team exit order, the base-pin combo are two of the key slots on a 10-man team. If the other members are good, they'll look great working on a good base. If you want to build a sub-20 second star, the base-pin needs to be superhuman at subterminal RW. That, plus starmastering and/or spotting, and the importance of their slots for speed put a lot of pressure on these two—so they must be cool under all conditions.

The base man does about 50 or 60 percent of the pinning. He doesn't "just lay there" or backslide, but works toward the pin who is descending on him rapidly. On speed stars this usually means that he glides along with the airplane after exit maintaining its speed so that he and the pin have a minimum of horizontal distance to cover. On really good speed star teams, the base man is an ace.

If you have a fast 10-man team, try putting four of the fastest men out first. Be sure they have good subterminal ability. Going out of a large door airplane requires an *instant* four-man because the "gob" exit puts everyone THERE. The challenge is to enter fast and smooth. To enter at all, you must have an open slot. To have *any* slots you must have an immediate two-man. To build a 15-sec. 10-man you must have a four-man in about seven seconds. If you don't think that is hard, try it.

Avoid forming or joining a team unless you have enough time and money to make a useful addition to the team.

Be sure the goal of the team is understood by everyone. It takes a long, long time to build a championship team. If your goal is limited only to winning—placing first and nothing else—then don't bother. Winning comes from doing good relative work with your teammates, and working with (not against) them. It comes from entering RW meets just for the practice of competition. Winning comes from everyone placing the strength of the team over their own ego.

Join a team to do good RW and to learn to do better RW. Join a team to have some fun along with a lot of work that will be challenging and satisfying. If you insist on "winning or nothing", try the individual events where your ravings won't hinder someone else's efforts.

Chapter XIII
How to Do Four-Way RW

 Four-way relative work is a specified set of maneuvers that is its own event in international competition. It preceded 10-way and 8-way competition at the national level because historically many small drop zones without large aircraft do have a four-place airplane. Four-way relative work provides intense, fast-moving skydives. It is the fastest way to learn how to do 8-way sequential relative work. And because it involves only four people, the dives are easier to organize and practice.

There is a growing repertoire of 4-way dives for the RW freak to whet his or her skills on. The list grows as fast as our numbers grow. The attainable 4-way dive is limited only by our collective imagination. Witness: sequential with more than a dozen maneuvers from 9500 ft . . . no-contact, no-grip, upside-down, three-dimensional, skydancing, looping cats, rolling diamonds, back-ins, backloop-sequential, vertical transitions, piece-flying, linked exits, free-flown exits, tag-team, horses, tube dives, or jousting . . . just to list some of the 4-way aerial dances going down at drop zones everywhere.

Getting Together as a Team—The Commitment

If you want to do some serious, hard-core RW . . . if you want to have a lot of fun . . . if you want to pick up a lot of RW technique in a short period of time, then get together with a 4-way team. You'll need three others

who are into the same thing you are, and then you'll
need a solemn commitment from each to:
1. Always be there for practice at the appointed
    time. Even if it is raining, be there.
2. Agree that during designated practice periods,
    4-way team jumps come first.
3. Always do at least five practice sessions on the
    ground before each jump.
4. Participate in a debriefing immediately after
    each jump, no matter how hot or tired you may
    be. This is where you figure out what you did,
    and what you'll do next time to make the transi-
    tions go smoother.
5. Apply enthusiasm and stick-to-it-ness. Deter-
    mine to make at least 30 practice jumps
    together.

Your first 10 jumps or so as a team may be disheart-
ening. It will seem impossible, but keep at it. Try to
think of ways to help the team work better together.
Soon it will begin to click.

You don't have to love your teammates. You don't
even have to like them, though it helps. You *do* have to
like jumping, because 4-way RW is a lot of jumping.
Four-way RW will make a flyer out of you. The things it
teaches you are subtle. You'll find yourself using techniques learned in 4-way on all your skydives.

Home planning sessions are a good place to start
getting it all together. If you are planning to compete,
every team member should be provided with a set of the
rules (USPA Part 55) and diagrams of the maneuvers.
Everybody on the team should think about the maneuvers and contribute their ideas on doing them. These
ideas all add up to a game plan. A master team logbook
is a definite advantage, though not a must.

After you've decided on the maneuvers and have
drawn them out, you and your teammates must figure
out the best way to fly the transitions between maneuvers. Decide how one formation flows most smoothly

into the next. Having "little man" cutouts is a big help in ground practice. Paste these on a piece of cardboard for each person. "Fly" the cutouts through each formation on the dive. This helps figure out the easiest way of accomplishing smooth and fast transitions. It also serves to help everyone learn the dive.

Now you're ready to "dirt dive." Start by simply walking through the sequence of formations in order twice. Don't worry about the transitions or grips just yet. Rather, concentrate on the basic formations themselves. After fixing them in your mind, refine the dive by working on transitions, flight paths, and grips. Think about staying in close to each other. Practice maintaining visual contact. Pay attention. What you practice on the ground will be what you do in the air, so eliminate unnecessary movement.

Skydives cost a lot of money; ground practice is free. If you expect your dives to go well in the air, you must practice them on the ground. It may be compared to soccer or football practice or any other team sport where coordinated interaction with one's teammates is required. You learn to work together on the ground so that every movement and maneuver becomes reflexive in the air.

Four-Way for Fun Skydiving
The same "serious" team techniques are also useful when applied to fun-jumping with three other people, especially if you intend to get the most from your skydiving dollar. The only difference is that your "commitment" is limited to only one dive—and that is to take it seriously and give it your best effort.

First you must select a set of formations for the dive. Usually it is best if one or two people figure out a complete dive and present it to the others. The planned dive should be illustrated and set down on paper. Learning the pattern and flow of the dive thoroughly on the ground is absolutely essential to performing it well in the air. You'll want to use all the teaching/learning tricks you can because "brain-locks," i.e. forgetting which maneuver comes next or not knowing where to fly, can turn a good skydive into chaotic confusion.

Ground practice will quickly point out any traffic problems that may pop up in the air, and will help put everybody's head in the same place. As you slowly walk through the jump, have someone count the seconds out loud; listen to the cadence. Imagine that you *are* in freefall. Don't build a formation in four seconds if you usually take eight to 10 seconds to do it in actual freefall.

Try a reasonable number of formations. Practicing too many maneuvers is unnecessarily confusing. Practicing eight maneuvers when your group of four has a maximum potential of completing three or four maneuvers is overkill and dangerous. You tend to want to complete the set you have practiced, even if you run out of altitude. Ground rush causes panic pulls and low openings, so include altitude checks, break-off signals, and tracking in every ground practice.

On the first walk-through, concentrate only on the formations themselves and in what order they come. Avoid talking; notice which grips you'll drop or pick up. Notice who is where in relation to you.

On subsequent walk-throughs, polish the transitions between formations. Think about which way you turn. Think about staying close on transitions. Think about the timing and flow of your movements as it relates to the planned sequence of maneuvers. Practice eye contact and awareness of what everybody else is doing. Do each maneuver the same way each time.

Break-off, track and pull patterns should be part of the dirt dive because, believe me, anyone can lose track of time and altitude on a hot skydive. Consider having someone pull out at 3500 ft. This is a proven altitude alarm which also removes one jumper from the opening area.

Walk through the planned dive several times until everyone is satisfied they know the dive. Don't be embarrassed to ask for another dirt dive. Don't ask for a dirt dive for anyone but yourself.

Suit up early enough to walk through the dive with gear on. Notice jumpsuit colors. On loads where there are similar jumpsuits, look for boots, rigs and helmet colors which will key your position. Run through at least one practice exit in the plane. Practice the exit count until everyone counts and moves together.

The Theory of the Exit

A typical 4-way exit from a Cessna will see a hanger dangling beneath the wing strut, holding on in the windblast. Next to him is the base facing forward, then the pin facing either forward or backward as preference dictates. With only one leg and arm in the door, hanging down the side of the plane as far as he can, is the number four man—the first one away.

He is the first one away because he is knocked from his position by the forceful exit of the base/pin. He must turn and float up into the base/pin. The hanger will drop off the strut and slowly dive-turn on the subterminal air to reach the base. Movements in subterminal RW are very slow. However, this allows a high rate of closure in docking.

Many teams launch their exit with a combined count and head nod. On receiving the "okay," the exit key raises his head back as he shouts "Ready!" Then nodding his head forward, he shouts "Go!" As his chin touches his chest, everyone launches... in unison.

In a free-flown, or unlinked exit, the base and pin must fight the temptation to hook up instantly. They should wait until the number three person is there, keeping eye contact all the while. A 3-way is a more stable platform than is a 2-way. Ideally, the third and fourth will dock simultaneously.

At the contact point, be sure your entry angle and docking will assist the entry of the other flyers. If you hit so as to push the formation or cause it to warp, it will certainly affect the speed and smoothness with which it is built. Meanwhile everyone is flying the formation, making sure it does not track forward or backward or turn.

The first formation takes time to build. No matter if you use a hooked-up (linked) exit or not, in competition you must spend time exhibiting a valid first formation. Of course in theory, the fastest (therefore, the best) way to build the first formation is to put it together in the plane and carry it pre-built away from the aircraft... the linked exit.

However good the speed potential of the linked exit is, for inexperienced relative workers the potential of a funnel is nearly as good. Unless you jump with a serious and experienced team, you should consider using an unlinked exit (free-flying the first formation).

To Hold On, Or Not To Hold On?

Before relative work had a name, skydivers would exit holding on to each other, usually by the hands. This was a giggle, but very hard to fly back then. Later on, exiting the airplane already hooked up was considered poor form. At that time, flying together was the goal; there was even resistance to exiting too close to one another since that made the flying "too easy."

Then RW Competition—jumping against a stopwatch—provided an environment where the ability to carry formations hooked up out the door won parachute meets for some teams. This added the aura of respectability to linked exits, and soon the skies were littered with them. It became possible to be a part of a large formation without knowing much of anything about flying simply by being able to exit holding on to people who could fly.

Exiting hooked up is neither good nor bad. It is a proven way for top ranking teams to win skydiving meets. It is also a proven way for casual teams to lose meets. The linked exit is part of jumping. Knowing when and where to use it is important.

Use the linked exit if your team has enough time to make the practice jumps required to make it work every time. If it doesn't work every time, a linked exit only serves to slow down the jump. If you can't make it work 100 percent, then it seems silly to use it in competition or on an important jump. An attempted linked exit that fails removes all chance for a fast, smooth first formation—whether it is in competition or the base for a large formation.

Free-flying the exit is the most reliable way to build a fast first formation on every jump. Free-flying means that although you may exit holding on for a fast exit, at some point you let go and fly free to dock and form the first formation.

To free-fly an exit, line up so that the exit provides each skydiver with wind to fly on immediately outside the aircraft. There are no weird contortions and strange body positions required. The free-flown exit tends to be smooth and consistent: a good platform from which to build multiple formations.

To decide whether your team should free-fly the exit or carry formations hooked up out the door, experiment with both. Have someone use a stopwatch to time the difference between the two exits. Use whichever way is fastest and works for you 100 percent of the time.

Chapter XIV
For the RW Novice

 When you're first starting to do large-star relative work your most fervent desire is to be included on eight-man and larger RW loads. You want to get your SCR and SCS and "do" large-star RW. But getting on a load is often a problem.

Most RW novices grossly overrate their own RW skill. Since the load manifestor doesn't share your ego-blindness, he may not be sympathetic.

Analyze *your* situation—can you come in third or fourth 90 per cent of the time on small star loads? If not, you lack the real qualifications for big star loads where the mental tension you place on yourself will degrade your RW performance to an unacceptable level. A realistic self-assessment of your actual RW proficiency level is the first step to "doing" large-star RW.

Check your log book. Divide your total number of RW jumps into your total number of *successful* RW jumps. The resulting percentage will give you an idea of your skill level. If it's less than 80 per cent, you need practice. That is, RW practice, not large-star RW practice.

Results of a Bad Entry.   Andy Keech.

RW Skill Test

Another RW skill test (which is also excellent practice for RW of any kind) incorporates the following maneuvers. Starting with the easier and progressing to the more difficult you should, on a 30-second delay, be able to:

Jump	Maneuver	Proficiency Recommended
1	Make contact with a novice who is already making controlled 30-second delays. Novices are hard to catch, since their RW skill is low.	90%
2	Make a two-man hookup with another RW novice; then separate and do a 360° turn, another hookup; repeat. Make three separate hookups from 7200 ft.	80%
3	2-man hookup, backloop, hookup, backloop...Make three hookups from 7200 ft. this way.	75%
4	3-man, backloop, 3-man, backloop...Twice from 7200 ft.	70%
5	Delay your exit from one to three seconds and still enter, or pin, cleanly from 7200 ft.	80%
6	Be part of a 4-man built in 12 sec. or less	65%

If you are proficient at the above, your RW skill will speak a lot more convincingly than your mouth and you'll find yourself on more and more large-star loads as your skill progresses.

Closed Loads

Sometimes when you are trying to do your thing … which happens to be RW … you find that you can't get on the kind of RW loads you want on. It nearly feels as if you're being persecuted.

But there are other reasons why a load may be "closed" to an RW novice. Conversation with serious competition team members may shed some light on the subject. Here are some typical comments from RW competitors:

"People don't realize that jumping with unknowns is scary. … (Like all of parachuting) RW is risky. To do hot RW you must have FAITH in everyone on the load. An 'unknown' can destroy you and/or the star … I've seen it happen."

"I spend a lot of time and a lot of money to be good enough to do RW well. When I go out and someone's bombed the star it makes me mad. You don't ever need to bomb a star. When I had RW learning problems I corrected them on small star loads. Everybody should do likewise."

"During the months before a big RW meet every competitor (unfortunately) goes nuts and nasty trying to get his act together for the meet. There's just no time for fun jumps … my pocketbook can only afford team jumps."

Perhaps you've done a lot of small-star relative work but are new to the big star arena. Or you may be visiting a different drop zone. Naturally you want to make a swoop and get in some good RW. In these cases you'll probably be asked what your qualifications are.

That's perfectly normal and prudent. If you're SCR/SCS, say so. If you've earned one of the 16 or larger patches, or jumped in RW competition, then mention that, too. If you don't have much big-star experience but are a 100%-er in a pin, 3rd or 4th position, tell the starmaster that.

Don't babble. Just state the facts. Let your RW speak for itself. Skill speaks loudest with silence. The starmaster will assign you a slot. Unless you can't handle it, take it and prepare to have fun.

You'll be up there doing something you love to do. You're not paying money to prove something or to "show them." The easiest thing to forget in such a situation is the fact that you jump for the joy of jumping.

The vibes emitted by a positive attitude will help everyone. Mainly though, you'll have a good time ... and even if it turns out to be just watching people fly around a tumbling base, it's something you can't see on television!

On a Big Star Load At Last!

If you happen to be a nervous novice here are some hints that may help you.

Where to Exit. When you first start doing RW from aircraft larger than you're used to, spend at least two jumps going last and not trying to get in. Just get the feel of the aircraft, the exit, tracking, etc. When you are comfortable try to go out 4th or 5th or 6th.

You'll be a bit too nervous to handle base-pin-3rd positions properly, and these are key to the whole jump. Also, these first three slots involve a lot of difficult sub-terminal RW. The star load depends on your getting in when you're supposed to. That's pressure you don't need.

Going seventh or later involves too much diving, tracking and high speed approaches—and not enough close-in RW and star flying. You want to learn large-star RW, not track for 20 seconds.

Going in the middle of the load gives you a lot of time to make a good, leisurely, skillful approach and entry. Additionally it gives you a margin for error so you can re-approach if you miss your first try.

No one expects you to be perfect right from the start. However, everyone does rightfully expect you to act sensibly and to place the integrity of the star above your own desire to "get in," to "be faster" or similar ego trips. If you do a good job and give it a well-controlled try, you'll be asked on more loads even if you don't always get in.

But bomb the star, approach too hot, go below and

loiter there, and you'll build a bad reputation long before you build a star. Exhibit self-control.

Listen! When you do get on a big RW load, listen closely to the starmaster. He will give you a flying assignment which you are expected to carry out. You will be judged on your ability to follow directions, so listen.

Do not talk too much on the ride up. You're probably tense enough and babbling just signals this to others. If you are talking, you can't be listening.

Dig the sky and the clouds. Clear your mind, put your will in control. Except for the number of participants, you are going up to do something you've done before—good relative work. Try to build a positive, relaxed attitude about it.

Making your Exit. Making your first several exits for big-star work can be unsettling. Exits are hard to control. If you let yourself get rattled by a bad exit, the rest of your jump reflects that state of mind. So do yourself a favor and remember that the exit is just part of a whole sequence of things that make up the jump.

Get solidly into the exit lineup. Concentrate on getting into the count and sway of it. First work on just getting out the door. If you hit the door jamb or "Z" out the door, resolve not to panic or overcompensate (overamp) on the rest of the jump.

When you find yourself outside the aircraft in the unfamiliar subterminal air, you'll have a tendency to "fight it" in your efforts to get squared away quickly. You may be confused because the Relative Wind is coming from the direction of the airplane's travel rather than from below as you'd expect. But if you stiffen your mind and body to "regain control," you'll lose the relaxed edge required for the rest of the jump.

Relaxing your entire body is the answer. Your arms, legs and torso will automatically find the direction of the Relative Wind for you just as feathers find it for a dart or an arrow.

Relax, let your mind take control, and you can begin doing the RW that you've worked so long to learn. And by not rushing to "catch up," you'll likely find that your entry time will be respectable anyway.

If you lose sight of the star because you've Z-ed out, don't get frantic. Relax. Go into a shallow dive, find the others on your load who are making a bee-line for the star, and follow them.

Approach. As you're aiming at the star, plan to stop dead still at a spot about 30 feet outside the star and off to one side. Be sure your stopping spot is about 15 to 20 ft. above the level of the star. Stop with a full flare, then begin a final approach to dock.

The reason for stopping is important. As a novice you don't have enough experience to know when you're in "full stop" in relation to the star. You'll tend to see movement as coming from the star and not from yourself. You have to *stop* to be sure—at least for your first few attempts. Otherwise you'll end up sliding around the star and you could bomb it...or someone near it.

You aim to the side of the star for the same reason. If you aim directly at the star and misjudge your stopping point by 10 feet, you'll likely sail right through the star. Maybe you won't hit anyone. Maybe you will.

If you stop 15 to 20 feet above the star, you'll retain some altitude to convert back into forward momentum to make a forceful and precise final approach without undue effect from the "burble," or wall of turbulent air around the star.

If you find yourself stuck in a slot and unable to lay your hands on wrists, going stiff and reaching for them won't help. You must flare up and back out of the slot so you can swoop in again with enough momentum to carry you onto wrists. You'll need to back at least eight feet out and six feet up to attempt a re-approach. Use a recovery position to accomplish this.

Docking and Entry. As a novice, touching wrists will at first send such a charge of adrenalin through you that you'll probably stiffen, float, and mess up.

When you dock on wrists or wherever, do not do anything else until you relax and settle to fly *with* the star.

A premature entry can endanger the star. A slow entry affects nothing except the traffic of others waiting to get in behind you. Since you're a novice, entering slowly and carefully is not only acceptable, it is preferred.

When you have a good, solid grip on a wrist or a jumpsuit, and are flying with the star, shake and break to enter. Now relax and dig it. (But don't forget that you still have to help fly the star.)

Break-off and Pull. At breakoff time ALWAYS do a 180° turn and track away from the star until opening time. To pull early, to fail to track away, or to track for the spot can easily get you killed or hurt. A large percentage of RW-related fatalities occur because of failure to get properly clear of the contact area.

At pull time ALWAYS give a wave-off and check around and above you before pulling. Do not sit up to pull, because you will backslide toward the contact area and a possible collision.

Do not pull above 3500 ft. Pulling higher on an RW load is dangerous and marks you as a nitwit. Pulling higher means everyone has to stop doing RW and worry about an open canopy in the area.

If someone in your area dumps while you're still in freefall, dive away from him immediately. If you've missed his body and canopy, wait until he gets line stretch before you pull. If you pull before he gets full line stretch, you could end up eating canopy. Remember that most canopies surge forward at peak opening pressure.

Once you have inflation, check around you for other open canopies. Have your hands on the toggles. Be ready to make a quick turn to avoid an entanglement.

Doing all of this is not hard if you've preconditioned yourself on other jumps and on the ground. Of course, the easiest thing to do in a tight situation is nothing. But remember, the easiest thing of all is to get killed. The important thing about proper break-off and pull procedures for RW is that you *do* them.

After the Jump. Don't expect everyone to feel the same way about the jump as you do. Some will be happy with their performance; others will be down because they feel they flew like turkeys. Only about a third of the jumpers will have actually seen what went on, and most of those will disagree on some points.

After an RW jump it's a good idea to listen to what other people on the load have to say. If you feel compelled to talk, remember that whatever you say is probably heavily influenced by the exciting things that went on, and that the resulting adrenalin rush reduces your ability to communicate courteously or completely.

To be more to the point: If you don't have anything positive to say, then *say nothing*. If you cannot come across with good vibes, then keep the negative things to yourself. Don't spit in the soup that you'll have to eat later.

If you really feel you have to bumrap the jump, it's a good idea to go pack your rig first. Then perhaps you can be more objective about it. Bad vibes is a sickness that can destroy teams, dropzones, friendships and fun. Is it worth it?

If you made a serious mistake on the jump you'll know it, of course, and you'll hear about it. But if you did okay, or didn't do as well as you'd wished and don't know why, then wait a bit, try to remember accurately everything that happened, and talk it over with one of the more experienced RW'ers who was on the load.

Jumping With a Team

As you gain more experience, you may decide to jump with a team, whether it be for serious competition or just for the security of always having a group of people to jump with.

Jumping with a team can be a very rewarding experience. You can learn much about RW by jumping with the same people most of the time—they'll be a constant against which you can practice your flying techniques. You'll be able to see more clearly, jump after jump, what your body is actually doing in relation to the others.

Every team jump is planned in advance. You'll take

your assigned place in the lineup on jump run, and your exit will be better because of your familiarity with the count and sway of the team.

Outside the plane, you'll always know where the star is and what your flight pattern should be. You'll be familiar with the falling speed of the star so that your flare point is not a matter of guesswork.

In the star, you'll feel the charge of good vibes that flows around the circle when you all know it's a good jump. The electricity of a team, trying its best to work together to build a fast star or an intricate formation, is very exciting.

Note: Portions of this chapter were specially rewritten for *Regnery Guide to Sport Parachuting*, published by Henry Regnery Company, Chicago. Copyright© 1974 by Charles W. Ryan.

16-Jewel.

Rande Deluca.

Chapter XV
For the RW Expert

 Freefall Relative Work is where it is today now. Later never exists and yesterday won't come again. RW just happened and grew. Being non-created, it is transcendent over acceptance or rejection. Unfettered, it does not ossify into ritual mechanistics and so continues to grow. Since it is represented and led by *participants* rather than a ground-hog "leader," it grows. If directed by a brotherhood of freefallers, this growth can strengthen us through unity in numbers. We are all just beginning. Let's begin together. Do some RW on the ground so we can do lots of it in the air.

Fundamental Courtesies of Relative Work

1. RW loads involve others beside yourself—be considerate of their time and their feelings.

2. It is impolite to be consistently late rigging up for a load so as to make others wait for you.

3. Enter the airplane in reverse exit order. Trying to reshuffle people in the proper exit lineup on jumprun is an unnecessary distraction.

4. The pilot is in command of the aircraft until jumprun and the "cut." He may need your help collecting tickets, shifting forward for take-off, etc. Help make his job easier.

5. ALWAYS give the countdown and exit your best effort. You may be good enough to loaf out the door, but it's not fair to impede those behind you. If you don't like fast exits, go last or as a floater where you are out of the way.

6. The integrity of the star is more important than your desire to get in fast. Don't bomb it. Get a *good* grip before entering.

7. If you go low, do not loiter beneath the approach area.

8. Always go for the assigned base man. If the pin man or someone else goes low, the star should not try to fly down to help him out.

9. Fly smoothly so as not to impede those behind you. Do not orbit the star in the approach area.

10. ALWAYS do a 180° turn and track away at break-off altitude. Look around you before you pull.

11. If you go low or can't get in, DO NOT pull high while the others are still linked in a star.

12. When you land, make it a rule never to bad-rap the jump you've just made. Others had fun, even if you didn't. Why spoil it for them?

13. There's a lot of adrenalin still in your system when you land. Use that energy to pack up for the next jump rather than to berate your fellow jumpers.

14. Remember, when someone makes a mistake they feel a lot worse about it than you do. Be gentle with the other person's ego.

15. Try to suppress *your* ego when you become a Skygod. Helping others to be as good as you are pays richer dividends than does creating tension. Remember that your SCR or SCS number, how many jumps you have, and/or how long you've been jumping don't really relate to doing relative work on your next jump.

16. Yesterday never returns; later never exists—do RW now!

The Etiquette of Large-Star Building

About 80 to 85 per cent of the large-star (16-man and larger) attempts made fall apart, or are taken out, by 6,000 ft. or higher. I can recall only a couple of large stars in which I've participated that were flown down to break-off altitude. Far too many shatter into so many one-man stars while there is still a good 20-30 seconds of working time left.

Since there are really only three major causes of small stars when you're trying for a BIG one, you would think people would learn, and after a suitable period of time, quit making the same mistakes over and over. They learn, but once they exit on the next attempt, they forget.

Here are the three biggest reasons for unsuccessful 16-man or larger star attempts:

1. Going too fast (over-amping, the ego—ME! I got in!!)
2. Going rigid in the star (becoming overly stiff, not flying the star properly.)
3. Lost grip.

These are such simple problems, so widely known, that enough people will downgrade the importance of these reasons on *your* big-star attempt so that you'll be tracking away by 6,000 ft., too.

Why do people get so gobbled up with ego or tension? Why do the people who build that all important 10-man base tense up? It shouldn't happen because it's something they've done perfectly countless times before. Why do the guys in the back of the load feel they must go so fast? They can do RW well or they wouldn't have been invited on the load. Failure to concentrate on their assigned job is the probable reason.

On a serious attempt for a 16-man or larger, the manifestors of the load know you can do RW well before your name goes on the list. The exit order is determined mainly by the 10-man base. You want the best, most solid 10-man base you can have. Often competition 10-man star teams base for large-star attempts. They can build a fast, sturdy, well-flown 10-man base formation under pressure; one which other select RW'ers can enter. Positions in the rest of the exit order are then assigned by someone who has an idea about the capabilities of those on the load.

After the manifesting, a meeting is usually called for all participants by the manifestor or starmaster. This meeting may take many forms, however, there are several key topics to be covered:

1. *The exit order.* Everyone should line up so they'll know who they follow.
2. *The countdown for exit.* This should be practiced by the first ten.

3. *Spotting and relay of signals to pilot.* Touch on this only briefly with the jumpers, but have a separate briefing for the pilot(s). This is particularly important if several aircraft are involved.
4. *Assigned entry quadrants of the star.*
5. *The Five Commandments of Large-Star Building.*
   a. Thou Shalt Exit Fast.
   b. Thou Shalt Fly SLOW.
   c. Thou Shalt Enter Cleanly.
   d. Thou Shalt Get a Good Grip.
   e. Thou Shalt Turn and TRACK at Breakoff.

It is very hard to get large groups of people together, particularly relative workers. Nevertheless, organization on large stars pays off, as evidenced by the tremendous amount of planning that resulted in California's 31-man star.

Organizers need just the right touch of authority and expertise. The first ten in the 31-man record were members of a competition 10-man team. Every individual on the load was capable of flying any position in the exit lineup. Each member of the 10-man base had the back of their helmets marked with a criss-cross of red tape. The second ten, marked similarly with yellow tape, were to enter between two reds.

The ever-present traffic problem was solved by giving everyone a consecutive number in the exit order. Even numbers were to approach from the right side; odd numbers from the left side.

To ensure good grips, each jumper had sewn an 8 to 10-inch length of flexible ⅝ths inch rubber hose inside the lower part of each arm bell of his jumpsuit.

Grips are especially important on a large-star attempt where a considerable amount of pressure may be put on the grips in a small area of the star. Because lost grips are a major cause of large-star failure, extra attention should be given to getting a firm grip before breaking into the star.

When making repeated jumps from 13,000 ft. above sea level or higher, it is important to recognize at the outset that most everyone will suffer from hypoxia. Participants should not move around unnecessarily. If you want to experience hypoxia, just try to whistle row-row-row-your-boat twice while at altitude. Hypoxia slows your thinking and reflexes, not the best conditions for building big stars.

There are two ways to measure the size of stars. The F.A.I. requires prior notification, and then observation of a star held a minimum of five seconds by an F.A.I. judge, for an "official" world record. The American rule is stated simply: "If it's not on film, then it's not a valid record size star."

The Tradition of Relative Work: Teaching It

Active relative workers are encouraged to improve and maintain the good vibes of RW. Your goal should be to promote parachuting in general, and relative work in particular. RW is a beautiful, exhilarating experience which you'll want to help others enjoy.

It took those of us who've been into RW for awhile a long time to learn it because there was no one to teach us. Because it was difficult for us to master, we sometimes forget that now we have the skills to teach this art to novices.

They'll learn much faster than we did because they won't make our mistakes. One of the quickest ways to build bigger stars is to have more qualified jumpers to build them.

In order to do relative work, you have to relate to others in the air. This has created a brotherhood of free-fallers. As brothers and sisters we should help each other, from the national and international level, all the way down to your group at the local DZ.

It's our sport. We must try to avoid ego trips, politics and hassles. We should promote those aspects of the sport which foster the brotherhood.

Every accomplished RW'er should work with novices to impart not only the mechanical skills required to fly the body, but also the attitude that releases the ecstasy of freefall relative work.

To do good relative work, you must have a fairly large group of proficient people to relate in freefall with. The better the overall RW level of your group, the better the RW you'll be able to participate in. This requires RW "skull" sessions and active training programs for RW novices.

As in any sport, there is a constant loss of participants who get married, move away, burn out, etc. Who will replace them? If it took you 300 jumps to learn RW, don't you now know enough to teach a novice in a lot less time? Want too build a 16-man star or a 16-man snowflake or some other presently out-of-reach goal at your DZ? Shouldn't you invest a little of your time in training others to do RW?

There is a natural Brotherhood of Relative Workers. We all work together to perform aerial artistry. Throughout history other groups have recognized their inherent brotherhood. They formalized it enough to keep the group strong, healthy, happy and growing. They laid down tenets of friendship, service, courtesy, hospitality, and training. The Masons, Elks, Shriners and others are good examples.

When you work with a novice, you're not just teaching the mechanics of flying—you're imparting a good, positive feeling toward your sport. You are hospitable and friendly to visitors and novices, not because you are basically a nice guy, but because you realize that only a big group of brothers in the sky can perform intricate large-star freefall relative work maneuvers successfully.

A very real problem, of course, is the novice with a big ego who won't see and won't listen. This case doesn't take instruction very well, and usually refuses to learn even the basic maneuvers. They're like the people who go to a movie and never see the picture.

My advice is to leave them to their own devices. Concentrate on someone who *wants* to learn. *Just five jumps with an interested novice will give him experience and knowledge of techniques that took you 50 jumps to learn.*

Do this in the spring, and you'll have your big dream star by fall. And, brother, you'll have a lot of fun getting there.

Working With the Novice Relative Worker

Here is a study plan you may use to teach relative work:

First, give the student a friendly, brief introduction to the art of freefall relative work. Anyone making controlled 30-second delays is a good candidate. Emphasize the beauty and things *you* like about RW. Tell him of the brotherhood he's about to join.

7500 Feet, Phase I. Prerequisites are enthusiasm for RW and ability to perform these basic freefall maneuvers:
1. Turns
2. Track
3. Clear (waveoff) to pull
4. Unpoised, bomb-out-the-door exits
5. Aircraft exit from the reserve "pin" position (facing the tail, his back to the strut of a Cessna-182)

7500 Feet, First RW Jump. The student's assignment is to concentrate on making a stable exit. He picks a heading and holds it. He thinks about relaxing; his seeing or not seeing the pin man (you) isn't as important as his relaxing and enjoying the jump. In fact, seeing the instructor should key and reinforce the student's will to relax his mind and body in order to fully enjoy his first closing, docking, and entry. The instructor concentrates on perfectly controlled, clean airwork. Do not pin the student until after terminal is reached. Make a nice, slow, clean entry if your novice is relaxed enough to allow it.

7500 Feet, Second RW Jump. The student's preliminary assignment is the same as above. After this hookup, the instructor tucks up and allows the student to level out the two-man. Time permitting, the instructor next spreads out and again allows the student to level it out. The purpose of this jump is to get the novice RW'er accustomed to the idea and mechanics of flying in contact with others. Smile.

7500 Feet, Third Jump. It starts just as do the first two. After the hookup the instructor raises one leg, turning the star. The student's assignment is to stop the turn and then reverse its direction.

7500 Feet, Fourth Jump. Again, hook up after terminal velocity has been reached. After the initial hookup, the instructor backs off ten feet and lets the student try to close for a possible second two-man. Discuss floating, vertical rate of descent, reverse arch, and the necessity to pull before impact.

7500 Feet, Phase II. Graduation from student to novice! Student exits second from the pin slot. The student does as much of the relative work as possible. If successful, repeat the fourth-jump maneuvers.

Here are some other suggestions for teaching relative work:

Ground practice is especially important to a novice so he will know before the jump what will happen and how to do his part. Cover the basics of doing RW one thing at a time. For example, the exit is important but a bad exit doesn't mess up an entire jump unless the novice lets it by over-reacting to it. It is but a single mistake that is only a part of the jump. Just call it the Great Chain of Creation, with interdependent links.

After the jump, ask the novice what he thought went on during the jump before you give your critique. This makes him think about it and gives you an idea how alert he is.

When criticizing RW performance on a jump, be SURE to mention those things done correctly. He even may not have been aware of what he was doing right. Most people respond well to praise and positive reinforcement, and since a lot of jumps are relived throughout the following week, it provides some positive thoughts to dwell on.

Novices like having three or four things planned for a jump: say a three-man, backloop, three-man; or break it into a line and fly it back together again. If the first three-man is fast you can use the rest of the jump for more learning, and if it is slow you still had a three-man!

No jump with a novice relative worker is a waste of either time or money, especially if he or she really wants the help. You have the ability to reveal one of life's great experiences—a very natural high—and you'll both dig it.

★   ★   ★

> *Relative work is "new"—we've hardly begun. If we start today to plant the seed for a growing tradition of friendship, we'll be able to reap the many pleasures of relating to others in the air for a long time to come.*
>
> *Every one of us is a one-man star. To build something bigger we must do relative work.*

Chapter XVI
Skydance Resonances

Echoes Behind
The Art of Freefall Relative Work

Like any other creative endeavor, the art of freefall relative work is not static. This chapter is devoted to discussion of phenomena, flying techniques, and concepts of successful relative work that have evolved since the first edition of this book was published in 1975. It is hoped that our sport will never see the end of new ideas and flights of fancy as we share the joy of freefall with more brothers and sisters who love the air.

PART 1: PERFECTING MOVEMENT

Flying around the sky, docking at will, frolicking among clouds... swooping in general is what skydiving is all about. Funny thing, though, it's all easier to talk about than to do. Unless you know two secrets, well, maybe three secrets.

In skydiving, there are two critical actions. First in importance is the ability to *not* move out of a vertical plane—the skill to fall straight down, and fly straight up.

As important as the up-down ability is, it begs the question of the second secret of relative work—how to move horizontally. The ability to move forward, backward and sideways at will is also the second of the two actions in skydiving.

Controlled movement comes from one thing. Movement in any horizontal direction in freefall is the result of using muscle tension. The key to flying across the sky is understanding that the more strength and energy you use, the more distance you will cover. To get there faster, you will have to push harder. If you aren't getting there soon enough, then you failed to push your arms and legs against the wind hard enough.

How hard must you push? Well, here is a direct example. Lie on the floor and do five push-ups (press-ups) now. NOW. Quit reading about it and get down there on the floor and DO it!

Stop still while only halfway down on the sixth push-up. Hold that position. Notice how after awhile your arms and chest feel sore? They're sore because you are pushing against the floor hard enough to "hurt." Notice the effort required to lift your body off the floor.

Now, while lying on your chest, place the top of your foot and ankle on a chair or sofa. Push with your legs until they are straight, lifting your lower body off the floor. This takes a fair amount of strength, right?

Finally, do a push-up while still supporting your ankles on the chair. Or, push/press on the floor and try a push-up. Hold what you get until you can clearly recognize which muscles you are using to hold yourself up. Notice which parts of your body supply the required push to lift you. Notice how hard you must push to stay up.

Next time you skydive, remember this experiment: whenever you want to move faster, use the same muscles to push harder.

If you're too slow getting there on time, or you can't stop quickly enough after a dive, or you can't gain altitude when you want to, or track faster than most of your friends . . . if you have those excuses for your sky-dives, then you are just not using your strength intelligently or adequately.

There is no limp-wristed, feeble, half-hearted approach to fast horizontal movement. Your speed is a result of how hard and effectively you push on the wind. If you aren't exhausted after a skydive, it may mean you didn't try hard enough. Or hopefully, it means instead that you didn't need to try hard because you've learned that it is easy.

Falling True, Falling Straight

The key to the secret of the art of relative work is in falling straight down. To fly true, crisp and clean, you must first master the technique of flying straight down. No slides, no weaves, no floats, no bobbles. No drifting; just directly *down.*

It's easy. In fact, it's the only way anyone ever gets good at the art of flight. Imagine with me a dirt-dive. There are you and I and about six or 50 of our friends. We're all sitting around in a group on the ground. We're each close enough to touch two or three mates. Of course, we're relaxed and happy.

Notice how easy it is to stay close when no one moves? Executing a 16-maneuver practice dirt-dive would be simple here on the ground as long as no one moves out of their position. Even a 34-sequence dance would be easy if we had a plan, and nobody moved.

Now, let's take our group upstairs to 12,500 ft. above the ground. Picture the same people, all together in the same places as before, except now we're in freefall. If each person keeps their position relative to each other perfectly, we can easily perform beautiful formations, sequences, and dances in the air. Suddenly, 10...16...34 or however many maneuvers you desire is attainable... *if everybody flies straight down.*

It's obvious the only reason we don't always get through all the maneuvers we've planned for a skydive is that we don't all stay in relative position. Flying any direction except straight down will quickly cause separation. Flying *nearly* straight down isn't good enough.

How to Master the Art of Flying Straight Down

Direct vertical flight is easy if you let the wind give you your own personal position. Take another look at the picture of the RW Stable on page 15 (Fig.8). Note that you allow the wind to mold you into the correct position; you do not "take" a position.

If you take a position you "think" will be best for you, then you will fail. But if you let the rushing air lift and form you according to your size and shape, then its lift will be exactly right for your jumpsuit, your body, and your fall-rate.

Said another way, if you assume a rigid position and ignore the effect of lift on your hands, feet, legs, torso, etc., you will have to expend a lot of energy just to stay in one place, i.e. fall straight down. You'll use up so much energy doing this that other RW flight is difficult, if not impossible. It's like trying to skydive holding on to a 4 ft. x 8 ft. tabletop. It will slide and skitter all around the sky uncontrollably.

To see for yourself, take a deck of ordinary playing cards and try to drop each card into a hat from a height of 6 ft. You'll be lucky if you can get even one card out of 52 to drop into the hat! Now, crumple a card into a wad. This wadded-up piece of paper will fall easily into the hat on the first try.

So, how do you learn to fly straight down? Start this way: Lie out flat on the floor, on your stomach. Imagine that a warm and friendly wind is supporting you. It's like you are floating at ease in a swimming pool, with the water gently supporting your body. Let the imaginary wind blow, lifting your arms into a very relaxed position. Let it lift your thighs and feet up to the normal position of freefall.

Soon you are floating on the air in a belly-down, relaxed position. Your spine is curved as your belly-button is pressed into the floor. Your shoulders are up and back, nearly trying to touch. Imagine that the wind has just draped you against a big beachball placed on your back. This is what the natural RW stable you must attain in freefall is like.

On a skydive, you do the same thing...let the wind mold you into your personal, wind-given RW position. This natural position is always the "best" one for you.

That's all there is to it . . . the key to clean, easy sequential RW is to be able to fall straight down. To fall straight down, all you have to do is relax on the wind and let it give to you your own personal, natural RW stable.

Now you're *really* riding the wind. Smile and go for it.

PART 2: RELATIVE FALL

Understanding that the key to clean relative work is developing the ability to fall straight down took a long time. It seems to ignore the most obvious aspect of skydiving . . . that falling together or flying relative to one another is the root of "relative" flying, hence relative work.

And, after you get down to a formation, you must then stay "relative" to it while you fly in to dock. A problem is that we often think we must use our arms and legs to "stay with" the formation. Poppycock!

Using your arms and legs for anything but horizontal movement, grips, wave-off, etc. is silly. Why? Because it ignores the best rate-of-fall control device ever invented: your torso.

Torso Flying

In order to move horizontally across the sky you must maximize use of your arms and legs. But, attempting to control your relative up and down altitude with your arms and legs is not as efficient as using your torso.

Your torso is your automatic elevator button. It is connected to your other button: your belly button. Here's how it works:

Stand in front of a full-length mirror wearing your gear. Notice your total surface area with arms and legs outstretched. Now consider the effective area of your torso, disregarding your arms from shoulder-seam to fingertips and your legs from crotch to toes.

There is a big chunk of body remaining! Your head, hips, stomach, chest and shoulders add up to an area nearly equaling the total area of your arms and legs combined. This is your torso. It is your key to flying in the up or down sense. Learn to use it.

Consider this: the RW stable is the fastest possible sink position. The reverse arch, or "recovery position," is the fastest way up. It follows, therefore, that when you want to sink down to something you must have your belly button out, your hips and shoulders thrown back, your spine bowed, your chin back. It is as if puppet strings were tied to your upper thighs, shoulders and head and pulled back until they touched. This is a *very* fast-fall position.

Likewise, when you want to float up to something or recover altitude, you must suck in your stomach and cock your hips, while you roll your shoulders forward and suck in your chest. Your chin should be tucked into your chest, and you must press on the wind. In this position you *will* go up, whether or not you use your arms and legs. (Using them, too, however, results in the fastest up position.)

The fast-fall position is a relaxed back bend. The slow-fall position uses a lot of strength to "cup" the torso. Or to go *down*, think "belly button OUT, shoulders/head/butt touch." For coming *up*, think "belly button IN, stomach/chest sucked in, shoulders/head/hips forward."

Unfortunately, many slender "feather-asses" frantically try to get down by tucking their elbows and knees close to their body. Pity . . . because by tucking in their arms and legs to get them out of the airstream, it's at the expense of having their torso in the slow-fall position! So they float, bobble about, and cannot settle in to fly with the formation.

In the same way, heavyweights try to fall slower and "stay level with it" by stretching out their arms and legs. Sometimes their stomach is out, too, and the wind blows them into a faster fall . . . so they sink out even further and go low.

The answer, then, whether you're heavy or slender, is to use your torso to give you a rate of fall that is compatible with the people you are jumping with.

If you jump a big-wing jumpsuit, you'll need

to match the lift of the wings by cupping your lower torso. This will lift up your ass and help keep you from backsliding.

Rate of Fall

The rate of fall must be fairly high (fast) for good RW. In the big jumpsuit era, everyone tried to fly at the outer limit of their flight envelope. Each flew as slowly as possible, attempting to "gain altitude" for the next sequence, or formation. The not-uncommon result of too slow a fall rate is people going low, incomplete skydives and dissatisfaction.

Good relative work requires that your rate of fall be fast enough to allow you to maintain a relaxed position and still have enough airspeed to maneuver cleanly.

A botched exit, bad entry or lost grip tends to make everyone tense. Tensing up makes skydivers float, and floating causes the formation to rise up until it self-destructs.

Because a fast fall rate is critical to the success of any skydive, the most experienced skydivers on the load should set the rate of fall fast enough to accomplish the planned maneuvers.

Next time someone "goes low" on one of your dives ask yourself, "Did they go low, or did the formation float up on them?" Nothing flies well without airspeed. Keep your airspeed up.

Where Is "Level?"

How does one define where level is in a skydive that looks like a swarm of summer gnats above a picnic? I mean, if you are a gnat wanting to convert the melee into a mega-blot sequencing into docking wedges, where is the level plane of the formation in the up-down sense? At the center, you say? Nope.

On organized skydives, a respected flyer in the core-group of the formation defines "level" by where he or she is. This reference-point person must make certain to be at the best place for everyone on the dive.

This is usually at a place below the center of the dispersed bodies, because flying down is easier than flying up.

This is called "centerpointing" if everyone flies the concept. The referent flyer always attempts to fly in perfect position.

Centerpointing and Perfect Position

Centerpointing is an art and a skill which, when used in conjunction with the idea of perfect position, leads to completions and successful skydives.

Perfect position means that after centerpointing, you take the position in the sky in relation to your mates that you will end up in when the desired formation is completed as planned.

In other words, if you will end up flying sideways to Jane, facing Fred and 5-1/2 ft. from Jerry's head, then you fly exactly to that position in the sky and orient yourself properly in relation to the others even if they haven't arrived at their places yet. Or, you fly perfect position so that others arriving simultaneously, or a bit later, do not have to move you around to assume their correct slot.

Centerpointing means that everyone notices each and every other person and their present position in the sky, and flies only the distance required to put themselves in perfect position and on time.

An example using a 5-way dive will illustrate these concepts:

The planned skydive: a linked exit, a 5-way star, 5-way donut, backloops, 5-way star, wave-off/track/pull. *The actual skydive:* a crummy exit that is spread out horizontally and vertically...people upside down, backwards and confused. The solution? CENTER-POINT... HO!

Steps in centerpointing, starting with the crummy exit:

1. Stop flailing; take a deep breath; smile.

2. Notice where the other four people are; make eye contact with each.
3. Without flying into the center, form a large no-contact star.
4. Get eye contact; breathe deeply; smile and smoothly fly to your perfect position, flying down about one meter while you do so.
5. Never form a 2-way star (they spin and slide). Rather, form an open star, leaving slots open for those yet to arrive.
6. Use only fingertip-light grips or no grips until everyone is there.
7. Hold the formation until it settles, or about two seconds, before keying the break to the donut . . . etc.

PART 3: NO-CONTACT RW

Feeling the air, sharpening your sense of buoyancy, noticing . . . and reacting to . . . the clues that add up to good relative work are happy experiences. If you'd like to increase your learning speed to the max, or simply enjoy the pleasure of some hot RW, then you should make some no-contact dives.

Regardless of your experience level, no-contact relative work is a great way to have fun and learn better flying skills all in one dive. You must be aware of the physical and mental clues to precision freefall if you are to know the perfection of flight. Flight for the joy of flying is what no-contact RW is all about, because you will spend the entire jump in precision flight.

No-contact RW forces you to fly stable. Everyone must be falling at the same relative speed, with no one stretched out in a recovery position or overly contorted to stay with the group. The test of good no-contact RW is to be able to touch your partner with your fingertips. Don't take a grip lest you spoil the no-contact flying for the rest of the flyers. Try to keep the distance between flyers as small and as constant as possible.

If you think you are good at relative work, go out with four or eight people and do some no-contact sequences. Try the international 4-way competition sequences, only do them no-contact. If you can complete four or five sequences from 12,500 ft., you are doing well.

When flying in the no-contact mode, be aware of the other people in your group. How can you alter your flying to help their flight? No one should be flying all stretched out in a maximum slow-fall, as this limits their control... and it's a lot less fun.

On the first no-contact skydive your group tries, you may need to form a contact star. Fly it until it falls straight with no tension; then gently release grips. Be careful that you do not push off. Fly into the imaginary center of the star until you could take up grips again, if you wanted to. Notice the electricity that builds around the circle. Don't forget to have fun!

No-contact RW requires that every flyer be aware of their own *and* everyone else's flight throughout the dive. There is a lot to be learned by watching and remembering how you and your partners handled the flight pattern of the dive.

No-Contact For Team Practice
Becoming expert at the basics is key to getting the most out of the learning opportunities offered by the team experience. You must practice timing and flow awareness, and no-contact is a good way to do this. Separate sets of sequential maneuvers done no-contact, side-by-side, are a good way for teams to improve group skills and cross-awareness. It's a challenge for each team member to learn to pay attention to what is going on around them.

Divide the team into two groups, each with the same number of people, and plan a dive for the number in each half. Alternate people from each group in the exit. Build the same formations side-by-side in the air, and execute the same sequences at the same time while maintaining 15-20 ft. of separation between the two groups. Do not let the groups get too close to each other.

For example, four people in two groups of two... each group executes in order and together in concert: a 2-way star, accordion, caterpillar, skirmish line, stairsteps, etc. With eight people, start with two 4-ways side-by-side, transitioning into 4-way diamonds, bipoles, donuts, caterpillars, etc.

Remember, this is not a race between the two groups. You're working on timing and cross-awareness.

PART 4: RHYTHM AND AWARENESS

Building awareness may start with becoming proficient at no-contact relative work, but it certainly doesn't end there. Rather, it grows along with your skill so that each experience offers an opportunity for sharpening your sense of buoyancy.

No-contact and sequential relative work both require multidimensional flying awareness. Keeping several formations, or pieces, flying together to sequence, rotate and dock with each other means that you must be aware of the flight pattern your formation must take to synergize with the others at some imaginary spot in the clear blue sky.

The ability to fly a formation precisely is directly related to being able to fly yourself precisely...and with happy imagination. You and the moving piece you are part of must flow as a complete unit.

Two and 4-way group flying builds awareness, so take every opportunity to incorporate them into your skydives. Practice pre-stars whenever the flow of the dive allows. Track the pieces away at break-off time as a last sequence. Practice group flying with the aim that you will not over fly your portion of the piece.

Timing and Flow

Good timing is the key to good relative work. Being aware of good timing is only part of the story, however. The whole book, chapter and verse, rests on being able to put that awareness of correct timing into practice in the air.

Perfect timing is being there, wherever *there* may be, at precisely the right time. Not half a second too early, nor half a second too late, but right on.

One gets there at the right time by flowing with the dive. A sequenced skydive goes only so fast, like a river. Rivers flow, carrying flotsam on their watery backs to highlight the currents. In freefall, the uprushing air creates torrents of wind in which we flow.

Being in your slot too early, before the formation has had a chance to settle and flow with you, causes waves and disturbances much like throwing a rock into a still pond. Flowing with the dive and entering with the flow causes nary a ripple. It is ultimately the fastest way to fly.

Flowing with the dive permits you to concentrate better on the changing panorama of the sky, ground, and sun-flashed colors of your dive partners.

Timing and flow start in the airplane, along with the rest of the jump. Whether building a subterminal donut, carrying a 4-way diamond out the door, exiting with a clean 7-way contact which sequences into a 10-way star still tilted on its side in sub-terminal air, or flying a 2-way cat out the door, you must start with a competition-style line up and exit, with timing executed flawlessly.

PART 5: VERTICAL MANEUVERS

Possessing skill in precise up-down flying pays off in many skydiving situations. Vertical maneuvers are easy once you understand the technique of torso flying. Using your torso to fly up and down with precision is most dramatically applied in vertical transitions and entries. While one advantage of good torso flying is that it gives you extra supercharged energy for grinning and waving at the camera, its most important advantage is that it allows you to dock on a formation from either above or below.

Vertical entries and transitions are used by many expert skydivers. It is a maneuver you don't hear talked about too much. Well done, it's so fast that few observers ever see it happen; but because a mistake could mean disaster, it is frowned on by many. Certainly there are jumps where vertical entries are foolish and not your privilege to attempt.

A good place to use a vertical entry is closing up the tail of a small diamond when speed is important. Done correctly, the tail executes a steep vertical approach into a fingertip docking, timed precisely at the same instant the last wing docks.

Trying the same approach on a caterpillar, however, is inviting disaster.

The idea behind a vertical approach is to stay high enough to maximize your potential for maneuvering, closing smoothly whilst going as fast as the flow of the dive allows. Said another way, don't waste any time getting there.

Vertical transitions—flying over rather than around people—are part of every good skydiver's bag of tricks. Start adding vertical movement over people to your skydives by planning practice dives that include them. Practice until they become second nature when the best way to get there is over someone.

Two to four people can practice flying over each other in leapfrog fashion. Include side hops and front hops. To leapfrog over someone, generate forward speed while gaining about four to six ft. of altitude, and simply sail over the top.

Any required turns can be executed in mid-hop. The vertical transition with 180 degree turn and entry is fun, but it requires a couple of feet more altitude for a safe margin of error.

Here is a skydance called "Elevator" designed to practice torso flying and vertical maneuvers:

Fig. 33
ELEVATOR

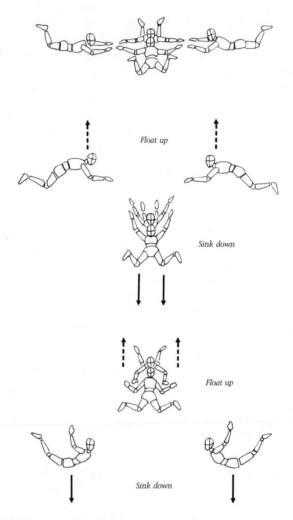

Fig. 33. Elevator.

Begin with a no-contact round; alternate flyers arch torso to drop down
about two ft., the others "get big" (de-arch torso) and go up about two ft.
Reverse: higher flyers drop down, lower flyers go up. Try to brush fingertips on passing each other in simultaneous up/down movement.

PART 6: FLYING BACKWARDS AND UPSIDE DOWN

Flying backwards is easier to do than it sounds. Once you've done a cleanly executed back-in, you'll always remember how to do it.

You're not really flying backwards when you do a back-in shot, of course. You're simply executing a well-timed, precise turn in place. The trick is to keep the backwards distance short. Rotate 180 degrees, close to the catchers of your slot.

To get a feel for the timing, walk across the room and flop down in a chair. Notice how you walk up, turn and sit all in one motion? Back-ins are done the same way.

When you start learning back-ins, fly up to your catcher, put either of your hands exactly where you want your knee to end up, and then turn and present your knee to the catcher's hand. Soon you'll be doing it so smoothly you won't even be thinking about these steps.

Actually, the real secret to back-ins is the catchers. A good catcher can handle fairly bad aim if he can reach for it without destroying the integrity of the rest of the formation. Since you'll probably pull it off satisfactorily, don't worry unnecessarily about your back-in. But because a clean, precise back-in always deserves praise, shoot your best shot.

Your catchers must be prepared as soon as possible, and the key to this is eye contact. Readiness is signaled to you by the catcher(s) looking into your eyes as you set up for the back-in and wait for their signal. Eye contact means "I see you; I am ready now." Catchers can do quite a bit of flying and passing of legs, if necessary. Be as smooth as you can. Remember to continue to fly with the formation throughout your turn and catch.

A real easy practice dive for back-ins is two of you alternating back-ins on each other.

Why Fly Upside-Down?

Why not? Flying upside-down is a beautiful visual

and sensual trip through the air. Everywhere you look there is blue sky, perhaps fluffy clouds. You feel as if you're in a new medium. Everything seems and feels different on an inverted skydive. Customary sensations are replaced by new ones.

Don't be surprised if your first attempts at going inverted prove difficult. After all, you've spent a lot of time learning *not* to fall back to earth. At first, just falling upside-down without popping over onto your stomach is a challenge. Making turns and moving seems awkward. You may save some money and ego damage if you practice the basics of a stable upside-down position and turns in a low-hassle manner— i.e., solo.

Polish your inverted flight techniques on other skydives whenever the situation safely allows it. You need other people in the air to relate to for feedback on turns and inverted moves. (Confide your intentions to a trusted friend so that your spastic flopping around can be explained to concerned observers.)

To build my skills and for a change of pace, I sometimes do inverted flight for just the front part of an otherwise normal skydive, going upside-down for the exit, descent and initial approach.

I exit inverted as a floater, flying to position upside-down, off to the side and slightly below a building formation. Being upside down, a normal approach from above would make visual contact a problem.

After getting into position, I go upright by doing an inverted front loop. This maneuver allows me to keep the formation in sight and is fun to perform. A barrel-roll is a faster method of returning to normal flight if time is a problem.

Upside-down flying can follow a normal right-side-up exit; however, inverted exits are a gas! Floaters can exit inverted without much problem after a few tries. Divers can do a slow roll in the first few seconds after exit.

When two or more people are doing inverted relative work together, the normal drill is to fly in feet first and dock with leglocks. To better understand this, lay on your back with your feet facing your partner(s). Bend your knees and spread your legs. Throw your arms back and support your shoulders so they are a foot or so off the ground.

Your hands are palms down; your arms are spread wide, supporting the weight of your upper body. Your chin is forward, nearly touching your chest. Raise your head until you can see your target between your knees. Your knees are bent with the back of your calves grabbing air for balance.

Flying inverted can be a lot of fun provided you open prior to impact. Take these factors into consideration in planning your upside-down dive—going inverted increases your rate of fall. Also, since there is some concern about the reliability of altimeters in an upside-down attitude, it is best to do your inverted flight routines at the top of a skydive.

Inverted flight teaches new skills and improves your ability to laugh at yourself. Have fun.

PART 7: FLYING PIECES

Flying pieces of formations (two or more people hooked up) as a single unit is interesting, exhilarating and fun. You can dock the pieces you fly together into new shapes. You can track a single piece across the sky. You can build several formations side-by-side, and then race each other to see which group can go farthest the fastest.

Watching another "flying piece" heading into yours for a dock is always exciting. The slow motion movement makes it seem like a ships-in-outer-space scene from a science fiction movie.

When flying group formations, the basic theories and techniques of working relative to each other are the same. Only our imaginations limit the size and movement of groups of two or more divers gripped together and flying as a single unit. The key to flying pieces is that all members of the group must fly as smoothly as if they were on their own. There are some special considerations of group flying to understand and remember.

It is hard to start a group moving. Compared to an individual body, groups or "pieces" flying together are hard to get rolling because inertia increases with the mass of the group. The more people flying linked together, the slower the starting movement will be.

Stopping movement takes longer, too. In this case, momentum increases with mass to make stopping "on a dime" difficult. Once initiated, turns are difficult to stop and require the focused attention of the entire group to accomplish them.

Starting and stopping a flying formation is the major responsibility of the person(s) on the tail. This is done primarily with the legs. To start movement, the legs are extended. Braking or stopping is accomplished by the tail person using an exaggerated knee-drop, like flaps on an airplane or the tail-feathers of a bird. (See Fig. 16 for an illustration of knee-braking.)

When braking, the tail person should drop below the formation slightly. For moving forward, he should be slightly above the group.

Turns are the major responsibility of the person(s) on the point of the formation. The most effective turn

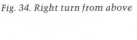

Fig. 34. *Right turn from above*

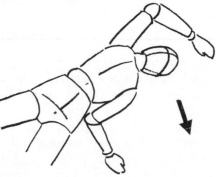

for the person up front is a "body turn." A body turn is accomplished by bending sideways and leaning into the turn. The arms will be asymmetrical. A normal relative work turn is not effective in group flying.

The "wing" people, or the divers on the edges or sides of the formation, can hinder or help movement. The trick to it is that the wing people on one side of the piece should work with the wing people on the other side, so that one side does not out-fly the other.

In a turn, the wing people on the inside of the turn should dig in with a knee (right knee for right turn) and pivot on a point, even backing up slightly. Those on the outside of the turn should extend arm and leg(s) to bring, or push, their side around. The tail will help determine at which point the group should pivot and use knees to adjust the turn. To stop the turn, the outside wings should begin the stop soon enough so that the turn is not overshot.

Everyone in the flying group must try to maintain as much eye contact as possible with the other group(s) of flyers. All groups, or pieces, should work toward the lowest one.

On docking, never fly your piece past the docking point if it will cause another group to have to fly further to dock. The dock should be simultaneous if there are more than two pieces to be docked, so as to avoid two docked groups floating above a third one which is on approach to dock.

Don't forget that grips in linked formations must never hinder another person's flying. Be careful where you take your grips. Simultaneous movement and grip changes are important to avoid uneven "waves" of movement that are often the cause of unplanned turns.

Finally, to track a piece, it is most effective to drive forward horizontally to gain speed. Often the tail flyer may be able to extend arms, Superman fashion, for additional forward drive. *Everyone* in the group must use their entire body in a track.

Some docks and dives to try:

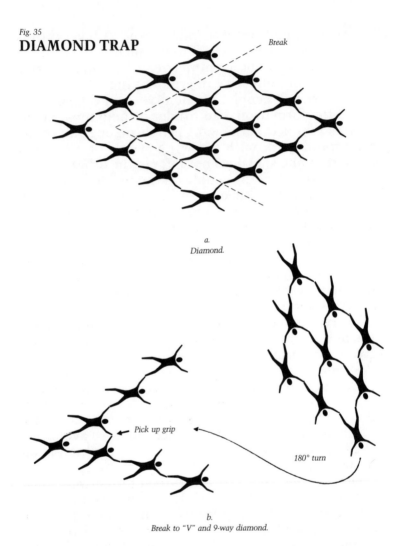

Fig. 35
DIAMOND TRAP

Break

a.
Diamond.

Pick up grip

180° turn

b.
Break to "V" and 9-way diamond.

Fig. 35. Diamond Trap.

*A good dive that teaches flying and turning larger pieces. The 7-way V for-
mation is fairly fragile, and everyone in it must work to prevent it from
distorting either horizontally or vertically. Turning the 9-way diamond
isn't difficult, but keeping it on the same level as the 7-way V requires con-*

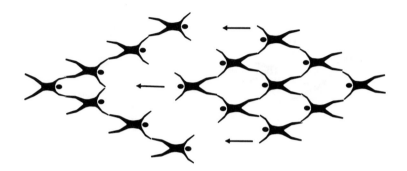

c.
Redock.

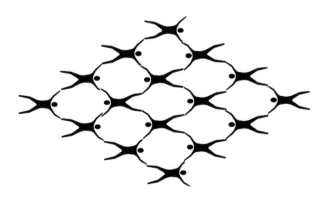

16-WAY

centration. To keep the diamond from turning past 180 degrees, start stopping the turn at least 45 degrees before the desired heading. Finally, to keep the two pieces from docking too hard, start stopping their forward motion while there is still plenty of separation—at least 15 feet—between the 9-diamond and the V. We did this dive in 1976 in Casa Grande, Arizona.

Fig. 36.

POTPOURRI

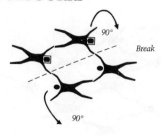

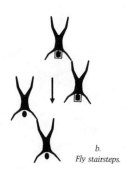

Break

a.
Opposed diamond.

b.
Fly stairsteps.

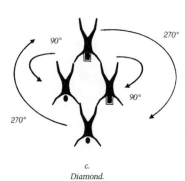

c.
Diamond.

d.
Four 1-ways.

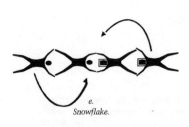

e.
Snowflake.

f.
No-contact round.

Fig. 37.
DIAMOND RACE

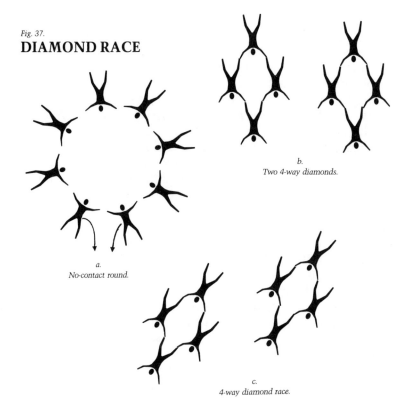

b.
Two 4-way diamonds.

a.
No-contact round.

c.
4-way diamond race.

Fig. 37. Diamond Race.

Executing this dive correctly is more difficult than its two points suggest. It requires concentration and awareness to build the two side-by-side diamonds on the same level without allowing them to drift apart. Tracking the diamonds away adds a bit of competition to the skydive.

PART 8: MEGA-MAN LOADS

Large formations are the ultimate challenge for many dive-planners. If you dream of a 50-way sequential dive, you are a Mega-Manic. You probably already know that realizing a completed formation is uncommon—many large formations are logged as "attempt," even with otherwise good skydivers. Why?

Time and distance on mega-dives mean they require different flight skills than in-place sequential.

Fast grip changes and center-pointing give way to high-speed swooping. Perception and timing is changed; even the air feels different.

Since the early 1970s, large formations have been considered a required item in every skydiver's credentials. Anything larger than 20 allows participants to walk taller. You've *done it*! You've *arrived*!

Large formations are generally built of wedge or diamond pieces for stability. For example, a 50-way formation is usually five 10-way wedges, or penta-wedges. Some cluster-type formations, usually called sunbursts, are used to accommodate various numbers of flyers in a large formation.

Fifty-ways and larger are usually built from an exit altitude of 15,000 ft. or above. Quadrant planning is easier if each wedge or diamond point person takes charge of their sub-formation for organizational purposes. Exit order assignments are easier if pinpointed on a large drawing of the completed formation. Thorough (and many) dirt-dives with complete briefings are necessary.

Because stability and a fast rate of fall are critical, today's mega-load planners have discovered what the mega-load planners in the days of large-round stars knew all along—that small jumpsuits with minimal excess wing are necessary, especially in the base and second wave or tiers. Flyers on the edges are still permitted large-winged jumpsuits, because going low and not being able to recover in time is a real problem as the formation nears completion.

Assigned Slots

It goes without saying that smooth-building large formations depend on everyone knowing their slot, finding it quickly and entering it directly. Nothing can screw up a mega-dive as easily as just one person in the wrong slot, unless it's someone orbiting the formation "looking" for their slot.

Whether you are assigned to dock as a wing, flaker or side shot, have a mental picture of your slot before you ever leave the airplane. What color jumpsuit is on your left? What color helmet is to your right? What kind of rig is in front of you?

The best time to set this picture firmly in your mind, of course, is the dirt dive. Gear up and walk through the dive on the ground from exit to pull at least a dozen times. Make sure everyone knows what to do.

After exit, fly directly to your slot and be set up on it slightly before you're needed, but not so that you cause a traffic jam. Never be too early. Never be too late. Be there on time and dock at exactly the right moment.

In larger formations you will want to enter your slot in a "wave" at the same time as others who have the same slot around the perimeter of the formation. This puts all of you out of the way for the next wave arriving at their slots. Also, by docking at the same time, the formation can't build too fast on one side so that it begins to float or self-destruct. The goal is to build the formation smoothly from the center out, without any part of it being built faster or slower than any other part.

Setting up in an orderly pattern around the base and not entering your slot until your counterparts on the other side of the formation can enter theirs requires discipline. Don't get tunnel vision. Be aware of the other flyers. Watch the formation build as a whole—not just the part where your slot is.

Mesh your approach with the flow of the dive. Do not improve your position at the expense of other flyers—don't become someone else's traffic problem. Leave your ego trip on the ground; large formations are built by skydivers working as a group, not as individual flyers.

As formations get larger they tend to float, so set up high enough on your slot to give yourself a cushion on a floating or turning base. While those in the base will be doing their best to minimize float, you should be ready to handle it if it does occur.

Easy Does It

A zero-momentum entry is critical on a mega-man load. Use it. Don't try to salvage a bad approach by hanging on, swinging into or climbing up legs into your slot. Let go and fly back into the formation.

If you have a leg grip, take it at the knee or on the side of the thigh. Never interfere with another's control surfaces. Likewise, arm grips in the base are stronger inside-elbow to inside-elbow, and the formation's symmetry is improved.

The formation's base must cross-reference the ground continuously and correct for turning and sliding. The simple secret to building a large formation successfully is for everyone to fly directly to the location in the sky where their position is, dock smoothly and stay there. This takes confidence and a belief that you can do whatever you can imagine doing in freefall. So, concentrate on your flying assignment with happy abandon, and if everyone else does too, it will go.

Break-Off

Flyers who go low on the attempt and cannot recover should stay in the area, separating when the others do. No one should track away until the prearranged break-off signal is given.

Break-off for most large formations is usually started at about 4500 to 5500 ft. Break-off may be initiated by a designated person in the base who waves a pilot chute to signal that it is time for the outermost tier of flyers to begin tracking away. Each outer tier turns and tracks away from the center for a predetermined number of seconds to pull at a predetermined altitude.

Those on the outer edges will track the farthest to pull at 2500 ft. or lower, while those in the base and nearer the center of the formation will track for only five to 10 seconds or so, opening at about 3500 to 4000 ft. This system works well to stage openings and minimize problems at pull-time.

Discipline is required for everyone taking part in a large formation attempt—most especially during break-off and pull. If you experience a malfunction requiring a cutaway, remember that there may be people directly below you, so look before you chop.

Debriefing

As soon as it is practical after landing, regroup and walk through the jump exactly as it happened. Use tact to analyze mistakes constructively. Emphasize the things that went well along with the things that didn't. Being able to give and receive constructive criticism is absolutely necessary. As individual egos are trimmed down, the flying abilities of the group improve. Think together, fly together, and if your goal is to build a mega-man load together, you will.

Common-Sense Rules for Being Part of a Mega-Man Load

If big loads are part of your jumping goals, here are more hints that have been passed down over years of attempts:

1. First (and key) ... be selected. Unless you are the organizer, you must be invited on the dive. Hopefully, you will be selected for your proven flight skills. Remember that you'll always overestimate your own skills. And, if you jump infrequently, you may be perceived as being less skilled than you deserve.

A 30-way is a big formation. However, 30 people is not a lot of skydivers when you consider the drawing power of a big dive. Naturally, others want on the load, too. This means they must displace someone to get a slot. If a bit of back stabbing and politics appear, remember the law of supply and demand.

Organizing a mega-way is a study in group politics. Lists, charts and diagrams must be drawn; commitments must be made, received and filed. Aircraft must be arranged, pilots coordinated, and so forth. If you can cope with the situation, then it won't hinder your flying. Accept it. And if you fly as well as you normally fly, you'll get into the formation.

2. Be current. Don't show up for the attempt with a month of cobwebs to blow out. You'll only do as well as your last 10 jumps indicate. And if you can't remember how they went, then you're not current.

3. Communicate clearly. First, to the organizers where you fly best. The front "base" slots are usually reserved for the most skilled mega-manics. If you are among the 10 most consistent jumpers on the load, then go in the base. If you can't handle a position later than tenth, then stand down from the attempt. It's simply *not* your privilege to screw up a dive for others because of selfish ego.

4. Be prompt. Pay up on request. Commit early, in writing if needed. Expect to be removed from the dive if you snooze on either of these.

5. Be on time. Show up an hour early on dive day... and 15 minutes early at all meetings. You should be replaced immediately by a qualified alternate if you are even "just a little" late. It's stupid to delay and confuse an entire attempt because you are not there on time.

6. Keep your mouth shut, even when you know everything. Offer your opinion only when invited by the organizers. Most comments made randomly are destructive in nature. In particular, do not voice your negative opinions about the dive, its organizers, or anyone on it. It's tough to be positive about such a difficult effort. Nevertheless, experience proves that the only certain way to complete a mega-dive is to ensure that everyone knows how easily it can be done and feels that he or she can and will do it.

7. Be still on the ride up. Sit quietly. Boisterous antics may signal your nervousness. Frequently, it is the bounce-around babblers who screw up the dive. While hypoxia is seldom noticed, it is always present above 13,000 ft. Noticed or not, hypoxia is a major factor on big dives. Talking and movement make it worse—and it affects everyone.

8. Fly straight to the formation. On your dive down to the formation, follow the "beehive" track of flyers leading there. Don't worry about a bad exit if you are in the last half of the load. You have time enough. If you get there early, set up high and away—far enough to never interfere with waves that precede yours.

If you are especially skilled, the across-then-down approach is a good alternate to the normal 45-degree approach. But if you are unfamiliar with the special needs of the vertical approach, don't use it on a big dive! While it is an excellent approach with many advantages for the skilled skydiver, the risks are higher, too.

Lastly, if you're not invited to participate on the big load, consider taking the weekend off and go fishing or kill rats. It is always hard to get jumps at a drop zone during a mega-man attempt weekend . . . whether you participate or not.

Remember that these loads are stressful. Big RW formations place head counts as a higher goal than most anything else in skydiving. For mega-ways, quantity is defined as a "quality" skydive. Since this is a temporary definition, it is certainly acceptable for mega-mania . . . but in moderation. (In excess, the rules of Darwin apply.)

So, as Jerry Bird says, "Exit fast, fly slow . . . We all know we can do it."

PART 9: EXITS FOR FLOATERS

Floaters may be part of an initial formation carried intact out the door or off the strut, or they may be individuals placed outside the airplane for the exit. If you've never tried floating, you should. Having the best visual position in the exit line up is just one of the rewards of floating.

Hanging outside the airplane, in the wild blue and roaring wind, you start your exit in sunlight and watch the whole thing as the dive flows together in vivid technicolor.

Floating eliminates the problem of instability in diving out the door into the windblast. You start off already in the windblast and work from there. Outside the airplane, you give your sky mates more room inside, putting the last diver closer to the door for faster exits.

Use as many floaters as you can reasonably fit outside the door of the airplane you're flying. Three people are average for a DC-3 or Twin Beech. A Cessna with a step can usually accommodate at least one floater. A Twin Otter can handle as many floaters as there are handholds for.

As the exit line up is announced on jump run, the floaters swing into position. Usually the back and middle floaters situate themselves first. Particularly outside a DC-3, the front floater will tend to get blown back onto the middle floater who can help leverage everyone into place. Once the floaters are set in place, the exit count quickly starts. The divers exit through the door as if the floaters weren't there.

Timing a Floating Exit

As a floater, keep your eyes and ears tuned for clues to the precise instant of exit. By leaving at the right time, floaters will be close to the base but on the side opposite the divers.

On exit, weather-vane into the propblast and adjust your angle of attack to move into proper position. If this is done within the first three seconds or so, a quick, clean docking is easy. Should you find yourself on the wrong side of the base, too close to the divers, sit up and present your chest to the propblast. This should move you right into position.

Timing is important here; if you start trying to sit up after you've cleared the propblast, you'll sink lower than the formation. Pay attention to the relative wind of exit, and use it.

Here are some other tips on floating:
1. Get outside and into position quickly.
2. Start with a good handhold and hug close to the fuselage. It helps to wear gloves for firm handholds.
3. Watch or listen to the count and go at precisely the same time as the base does.
4. Keep your eye on the base. If you are not in position, react immediately. Good timing on exit assures a good position in the air.
5. Remember that "up" and "down" are different on exit from what they become after the relative wind shifts from a horizontal direction of flight (from the propblast) to the vertical, or from the Earth. Use this knowledge and fly on it.

PART 10: THE STEPS TO SUCCESSFUL SKYDANCING

Progressive relative work is skydiving not governed by "rules"—imaginative and inventive flight for the pure joy of it.

Progressive RW includes but is not limited to symbiosis, skydancing, 3-D, medley, innovative exits, floaters, awareness and flow, sequential of all types except that dictated by competition rules, upside-down flying, leglocks, no-contact, etc. Mainly, it is whatever *your* imagination leads you to do for freefall fun.

Let's take skydancing, for example. The word itself means different things to different people. It's been around for awhile—Skratch Garrison was practicing skydancing in the early 1970's. To my mind, the most rewarding skydancing is "medley," i.e. several skydances on one dive.

An example is a star-dance-star. This three-dance medley is called "Oreo Cookie" because, like the one with two chocolate ends and a creamy center, you start with a circle, end with a circle, and there's lots of good stuff in between. O (a star)... a skydance of your choice... then RE-O (another star) before breakoff... get it?

Here's another example; it's called "Music" because the key to doing it is the beat of the rhythm that results from the flow of the dive happening right there in front of you:

The Recipe for "Music"

Requirements: 16 skydivers and 12,500 ft. of blue sky. Mix with a DC-3; allow to cook. Hot skydive...feel good! Exit fast using lots of floaters. Alternate exit order to build two 8-way stars 15 to 20 ft. apart. Complete break of all grips is signaled when both 8-way stars are complete and mellow. On the break, when everyone drops grips, the music begins.

The Dance: At the start of the music two no-grip, 8-way stars turn to face a common center. On the first beat all dancers move toward the next formation. This is a bipole in the center of two 6-way wedges, held for *one beat* before moving on to the next formation.

Keep up the rhythm with a snappy beat so you can get finished before wave-off time. Sequence of formations: two 8-way stars; one bipole flanked by two 6-way wedges; one 8-way jewel base flanked by 4-way diamonds or bipole flakes; two each 2-way caterpillars flanking one 12-way jewel base; 16-way jewel (or bipole-donut). Season to taste.

Maybe you'd rather start with a skydance for fewer people. Here's one to try:

A Recipe for Four-Way Fun

Requirements: four skydancers and blue sky. Combine with dirt dives, altitude awareness, and a healthy dose of good attitude.

The Dance: From a 4-way, no-contact star fly two to the center, do-si-do on your right hand and back to a gripped star. Go no-contact and left-hand partners repeat. Then, all to the center in a 4-way star; mellow it out till all smile; slowly invert until falling butt to earth, legs entwined. Grin, giggle and make silly grunting sounds such as a rabid horny gorilla might make. Track off, giggle, pull.

> *THE FIRST RULE OF PROGRESSIVE RELATIVE WORK:*
>
> *RULE #1. There shall be no rules for progressive relative work whatsoever.*

Skydance for Teaching Basic Freefall Skills

Instructors, if you're training freefall students, you'll find that skydancing is ideal for groups of two to four, five or six. Students seem to be more relaxed when they don't have to worry about connecting with someone physically. Best of all, it's easy to keep an eye on everyone in a skydance.

A simple dive that permits you to be in the air with four novices and assess everyone's flying skills at the same time is a variation of the Spider Dance (see Fig. 47).

The instructor stays in the center slot, keying with a nod for everyone to move in the same direction to the next slot. It is not necessary for every flyer to have reached their slot before giving the next key. If one "falls out," keep the rhythm going; the missing flyer can assume position when ready without feeling the pressure of having to "be there" for everyone else to continue.

Skydancing has the same conventions as any other form of dance. In an ensemble, if a dancer gets out of position or misses a beat, the rest of the group keeps dancing. The "out" person rejoins the dance as soon as they are able. In the same way, if you were to stumble on a nightclub dance floor, you'd simply recover and rejoin the dance. The music doesn't stop. The other dancers never pause; they don't have to stop and wait for you. The same is true in skydancing. A donut with one person missing is still a donut... with one empty slot.

A good skydance for teaching cross-awareness and gentle grips is a variation on Swinging Gate (see Fig. 46) that I call "patty-cake." Everyone turns first to their left, then to their right, "patting" each other's palms gently (no grips!)

Here is another basic skill-builder for three to five novices that uses two instructors. Learners usually go bonkers on this one because of all the flying time:

Fig. 38.
RED ROVER

Set-up area

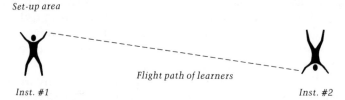

Flight path of learners

Inst. #1   Inst. #2

Two instructors, or skilled relative workers who want to practice an in-place vertical position, set up 20 ft. apart facing in opposite directions. They must maintain visual contact to keep from drifting apart while providing a focal point for the other flyers.

Flyers first set up on instructor #1, getting as close as they can, and then promptly fly over to set up on instructor #2, then back to #1, and so on. If they can, novices may fly up and tag the instructor's hand as they fly back and forth, but it's not necessary.

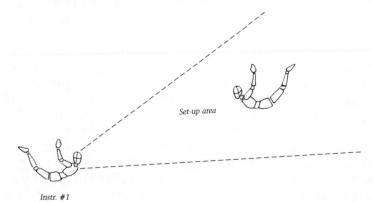

Set-up area

Instr. #1

Dance Master's Cookbook for Tasty Skydives

Always remember that skydancing is more of an art form than a competition for time or completeness. Since your goal is to have fun, use plenty of imagination. Direct your thoughts toward visualizing a line of energy that runs from your belly button along the path of perfect flight, and follow it reflexively.

Or, produce a movie of yourself in your head—a movie in which you make the most beautiful and perfectly flowing approach possible. Following your own lead, flow with the image into position. Relax, rest on the wind, and orchestrate its flow. Let the movement of the target suggest your moves for a smooth mesh with the skydive, and a feather-touch dock.

The following thoughts on skydancing are from Diana Rowland. Diana and I put together a skydance team at Perris Valley in 1979 or so. We wanted to explore the possibilities of freefall in the context of fun and rhythmic ballet. Both of us were the choreographers; because she has good rhythm, Diana was the "dance master" who kept the beat, much like an orchestra conductor.

Coca-Cola, the 1987 French national 4-way champions.   *Van Wideman*

We called our team "4-Play: Skydance Medley"...
eventually we had 10 members and color-coded jumpsuits with large visible numbers on the sleeves. Diana
put some of what we learned down on paper:

In traditional relative work, movement is a means
to an end—completing a formation. In skydancing, the
movement is an end in itself; the goal is flight for the
joy of flying. The aim of all flight is to make it smooth
and flowing, stopping only to prepare for the next
movement. This allows you to maximize the freefall
time of a skydive by using it all for flight, rather than
sitting in a static formation.

Besides the sheer joy of constant flight, there are
other benefits to be reaped from skydancing. Since skydancing is primarily no-contact, you'll find that your
skill in such essential things as falling straight down
will be greatly improved. You will never again have to
"hang on" to a formation. You'll also find that you gain
speed, because the fastest flight is smooth flight.

Skydance is just what it says. It's a dance in the
sky. Every dance has a rhythm, even if it doesn't have a
melody. And every rhythm has an accent per so many
beats; this is the pulse, or cadence, of the skydance.

Three-quarter time, which is waltz time, seems to
go well with skydance. Three-quarter time means there
are three beats per measure with the accent on the first
beat: *1'*-2-3. *1'*-2-3. Now to utilize this in your dive, you
should start each movement on the accent or beginning
of a measure and end each movement on an accent.
Then hold or sustain this position for the remainder of
the measure.

For example, take four people doing Donut Madness. From a 4-way, no-contact star everyone turns slowly 90 degrees to the right counting slowly *1'-2-3*. As you arrive in position, say *1'* again and hold for 2-3. You may fingertip the jumpsuit of the leg in front of you, but don't take a grip! Instead, concentrate on being parallel to the body across from you and squaring it off (it's a ox—not a jelly doughnut).

Now, feeling the flow, everyone turns to the left, going slowly through a no-contact star to a no-contact donut in the other direction. This would again be counted *1'-2-3* and held for *1'-2-3*. Do this for a whole dive, or plan to eliminate the sustained measure halfway through.

When you feel accomplished at this, try Pandora's Box. Begin the same as above, turning from a no-contact star 90 degrees to the right *1'-2-3*, hold *1'-2-3*. Then continue turning right (yes, that means you're all turning *away* from the center!) slowly going through a 4-way, no-contact back-in *1'-2-3*, to a no-contact donut in the opposite direction. Hold *1'-2-3*, then turn again to the outside and back to the first donut.

You may be surprised as you discover your inability to fall straight down while turning in place. (That's why it's called Pandora's Box.) Remember to square it off each time, flying parallel to your counterpart. If you find this too difficult at first, turn just two people at a time, letting the other two be your point of reference.

It's fun discovering your own creative ability to design dances that meet you and your friends' needs for skill-building, laugh-producing skydances. Here are some points to keep in mind:

1. Flow is more important than completion.
2. You can construct dives around ad-lib and spontaneity. For example, plan nothing but to come back to a no-contact star at some sort of slow rhythm, and let each person do what they want in-between (things such as back-loops, back-ins, somersaults, imitating or hopping over his neighbor).
3. Take time to smile and be aware you're dancing and flying with your friends.
4. Remember to open your eyes and expand your awareness to take in everything ... ALL the jumpers ... the ground ... clouds ... rate of descent ... and the flow of the dive. Use your sixth and seventh senses that you forget to use on the ground to perceive what you can't see.
5. A skydive starts on the ground. Don't waste your dirt dives. Don't waste the plane ride up either. Use your power of visualization (autogenics) to see yourself going through a perfect dive—from exit to opening—being as graceful as a combination of Baryshnikov and a Golden Eagle.
6. The better shape you're in, the better flyer you'll be. Don't forget to do limbering exercises either.

In addition to rhythm, most dances have a melody that adds to the flow. To utilize this, you may want to get everybody humming the same tune during the dirt dive. Or bring out a tape recorder or a guitar. You'll be amazed at how this improves concentration and cuts down the chatter on dirt dives. Then go up and try to dance to this piece of music the way you practiced it on the ground.

Don't forget to listen to the music, and have a good time!"

* * *

Here are 4-Play's favorite skydances. We did them with four, six or eight people. Notice that most begin after a no-contact "O" . . . don't forget to "RE-O" at about 4500 to 5500 ft.

DONUT MADNESS

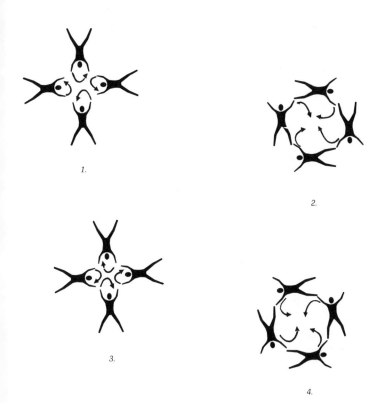

Fig. 39. Donut Madness.

Teaches donuts, in-place turns, group awareness. After an initial star, make it no-contact. Turn 90 degrees left or right to a donut, then briefly back to center, then turn in opposite direction to another donut. Repeat. Repeat. Strive for smooth donut-to-donut flow in a two-beat rhythm with the accent on the donut (donut'-star, donut'-star, etc.

Fig. 40.

PANDORA'S BOX

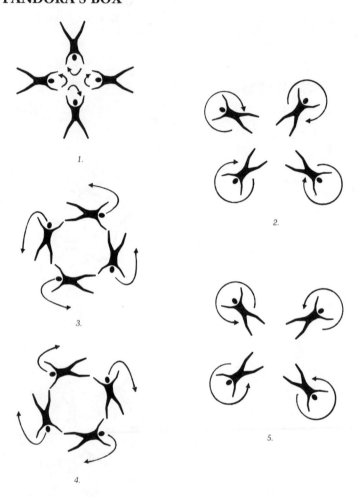

Fig. 40. Pandora's Box.

*Teaches in-place turns, perfect position, blind turns, cross awareness.
After an initial star, make it no-contact. Turn 90 degrees left or right to
a donut, then 180 degrees to outside for an opposite facing donut, then
another 180 degrees outside turn back in the opposite direction.
Repeat. Keep eyes to the center when possible. Strive for continuous
flow—more important than completion.*

Fig. 41.
360 + DONUT

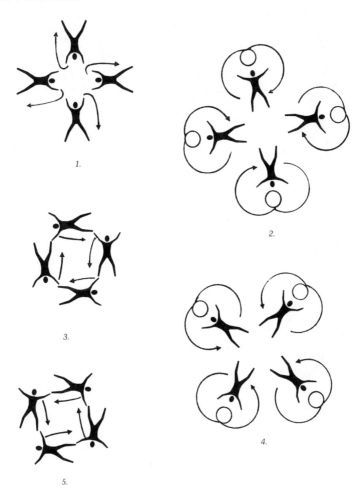

Fig. 41. 360 + Donut.

Teaches confidence, advanced blind turns, group awareness, rate of fall/radius of turn. Similar to Pandora's Box, but after initial no-contact star and first 180 degrees donut, continue 360 degrees more before donutizing. Reverse: 360 degrees turn and continue 180 degrees more to face the opposite direction.

Fig. 42.
CAT-FROG

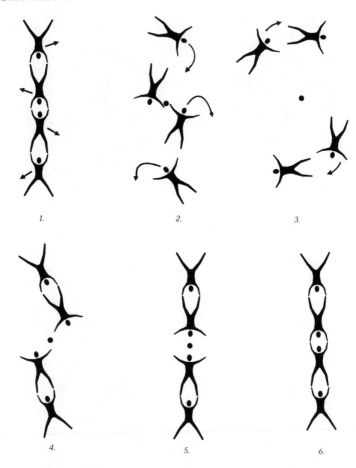

Fig. 42. Cat Frog.

Teaches piece flying, leg grips, coordinated turns. Brief star, then begin with a snowflake. After a total break, flakers turn slowly to their left almost 90 degrees, maintaining centerpoint and eye contact. Base people turn right 360 degrees, picking up the legs of the flakers on their way past. Meanwhile, flakers "back in" to center so there is a moment when all cats face out from center. The new cats continue turning as a unit until facing each other to dock again in a snowflake with a new center. As flakers become base people, it is their job to centerpoint, keeping eye contact and staying close to the other pair. Repeat. Cat-Frog can be done with any even number of flyers.

Fig. 43.
SNOWLOOPS

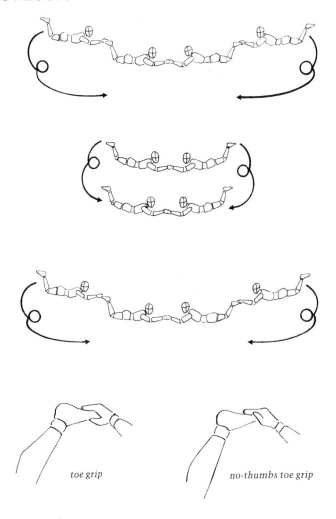

toe grip

no-thumbs toe grip

Fig. 43. Snowloops.

Teaches toe grips, backloops, vertical transitions. Begin with a snowflake—flakers taking toe grips, putting them slightly above the base. Flakers backloop in place, reforming as base 4-5 ft. below. Original base backloops in place and picks up toe grips as flakers on the new base. Continue backlooping and reforming.

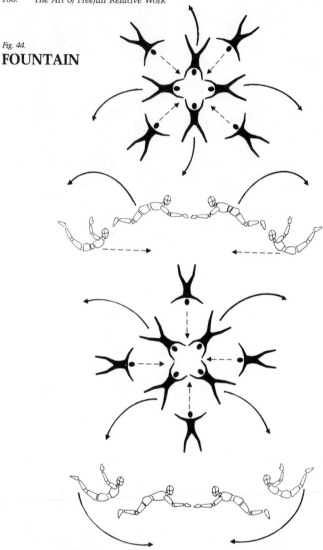

Fig. 44.
FOUNTAIN

Fig. 44. Fountain.

Teaches vertical transitions, burbles, rate of fall. Begin with a no-contact star. Alternate slots, move into the center and without making contact, float up, out, then drop down, setting up 3-4 ft. below the others. Remaining slots follow, moving into center, floating up and out, dropping to set up below the previous group. Aim for a constant flowing motion. Setting up 3-4 ft. below provides a reference point and helps maintain a good rate of fall. Beware of the tendency to float the whole thing.

Fig. 45.
PULSAR

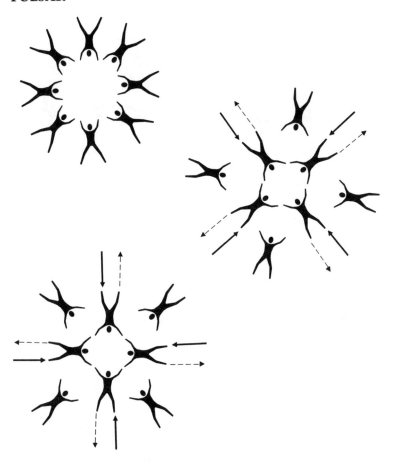

Fig. 45. Pulsar.

Teaches confusion reduction, memory. Begin with an even number of people in a no-contact star. As alternate slots move into the center (centerpoint), the others back out. To maintain a good rate of fall, flyers moving toward the center should also move down about 3 ft., allowing the outside slots some maneuvering altitude. Variations may be different center formations, and/or straight-in or turning movement. Rhythmic in/out flow is more important than completion.

Fig. 46.
TWIRLING DERVISH

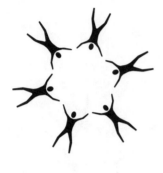

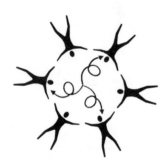

Fig. 46. Twirling Dervish.

Teaches turning entry docks, rate of fall in turns. From a no-contact star, alternate slots each turn 360 degrees into the center for a one-beat pause, and then 360 degrees out. Repeat with other flyers. Maintain centerpoint.

Fig. 47.
ROTATING SLOTS

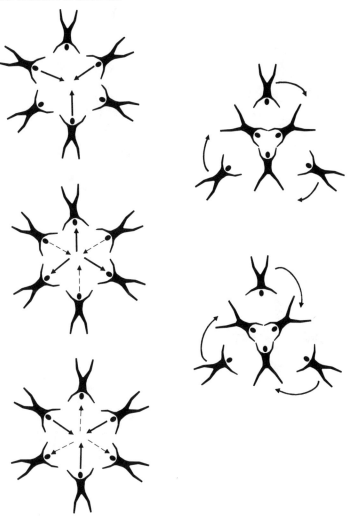

Fig. 47. Rotating Slots.

Teaches flying a star, flying a slot. Begin with a no-contact star. Alternate slots move to center for a contact star, and then rotate one-half slot to the right. Simultaneously, outside slots move one-half slot to the left (opposite direction); then move to center as other flyers move out. Repeat.

Fig. 48.
SWINGING GATE

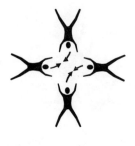

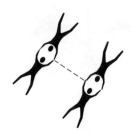

Fig. 48. Swinging Gate.

Teaches in-place turns, cross-awareness, fingertip grips. Begin with four flyers in a no-contact star. Pair off, making brief contact while keeping your eyes on the other pair. Then turn to the person on your other side for brief contact. Repeat, while keeping cross-awareness and eye contact, always with the "other pair," to maintain horizontal and vertical proximity.

Fig. 49.
HEAD-STAR

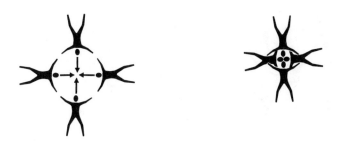

Fig. 49. Head Star.

Teaches no-contact confidence, rate of fall. From a no-contact star, gradually move in until everyone's head touches. Arms are relaxed and will overlap. Begin or end your skydances with a Head-Star—talk to each other!

SLALOM

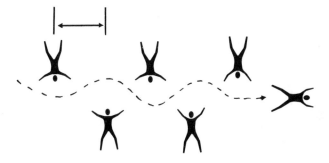

Fig. 50. Slalom.

Teaches station-keeping, group awareness. Flyers set up 6 ft. from each other as pylons in two facing lines. Facing lines are offset, about 3-4 ft. apart. The first flyer "races the course" and sets up as a pylon at the end; other pylons follow in turn. Maintain eye contact.

Fig. 50.
SPIDER DANCE

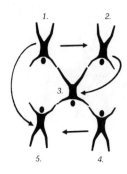

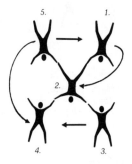

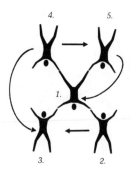

Fig. 51. Spider Dance.

Teaches confidence, key RW moves, tensionless grips. Begin with a spi-
der, either no-contact or fingertip grips. Following the sequence of
arrows, flyers move simultaneously one slot on the spider, always fol-
lowing the same person. Each move is keyed by the center flyer.

Fig. 51.
DO·SI·DO

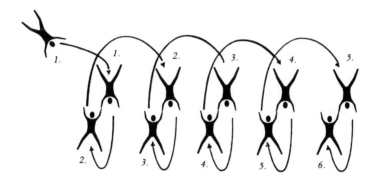

Fig. 52. Do-Si-Do.

Teaches piece flying, zipper turns. Flyers set up 6 ft. apart in a line, all facing the same direction. Flyer #1 flies to #2. Touching hands, they twirl as a unit 180 degrees. #1 remains in place while #2 flies on to #3 to twirl 180 degrees. #2 remains and #3 flies to #4, etc.

If all this seems difficult

If you've just waded through all this and still think that progressive relative work is only for the advanced skydivers at the big-name drop zones... If you believe that your friends can't do it out of your small airplane at your small airfield... then you need an attitude adjustment. Your head is screwed on wrong.

A small group of friends and a four-place airplane add up to some of the best jumping experiences I ever encountered in 20+ years in skydiving. If the jumpers apply themselves and stick to it, it always works. It's even almost easy, especially considering the fun to be had.

How you get started and what you do all depends on you. One important thing to remember is that you have to do these dives *at least twice*. The first time establishes the tone and sets the rhythm so you can "hear" the music; the second time, you dance.

Starting with the basics outlined here, you can think up flights of fancy of your own to perform in the sky. Use your imagination; there are no other limits! Imagine it, then jump it. Foster good vibes; express your joy through your skydives. Make a lot of jumps— then reread this book for a different message.

In conclusion, here are the simple basics for progressive relative work for four flyers:

- Pick maneuvers that match the ability of those on the load. Use diagrams and formation plays found in this book or *United We Fall*, your own dive book, cardboard cutouts or a formation stamp to make diagrams of your dive. If you're planning several formations, make the first one easy to accomplish.
- Work with four people who can all fall at the same relative speed. This is the key to learning a lot of flying in a short time with the least amount of hassle. Although most beginning flyers want to skydive with as many people as the air can hold, smaller groups permit the

fast learning and challenge we all ultimately strive for.

- Four-way formations are the basic building blocks for most RW sequences and maneuvers. These are diamonds (facing and opposed), bipole (4-way in-out), the donut, the snowflake, the compressed accordion, the stairstep, the star, and variations such as the "Y" and "T."

- No-contact and no-grip formations, while not easy at first, are a fast way to learn awareness and perfect position.

- In determining positions for the base, use experienced people who can build it fast and solid. Put the less experienced flyers on the outside edges. The practice of putting the turkeys in the front of the load has never worked.

- Design an exit that is as fast and efficient as possible. Plan to use floaters effectively.

- Each diver should fly to their designated spot in the sky and stop there. This may require flying sideways, even backwards, for some; others will fly no-grip until their connector joins them. This method of "being there" demands right-on approaches and fingertip docks. Perfect position avoids the chaos of grappling, lunges, grabbing and swinging on—maneuvers which seldom, if ever, work.

Pat and Jan Works.

About The Author

Pat Works has made more than 2800 skydives, and has been a member of the United States Parachute Association for 25 years. His interests include imaginative freefall relative work, serious competition jumping, teaching skydiving to others, and the preservation of sport parachuting through USPA. He was elected to serve three terms as a National Director on USPA's Board of Directors (1980 through 1986).

As a relative work trainer, Pat developed an instruction method combining classroom lectures and practice jumps to communicate basic skydiving techniques quickly, safely and with an attitude of joy in flight. He has conducted relative work training camps in France (1976), West Germany (1978-1980), Hawaii (1981), England (1979) and at Perris Valley Paracenter in California (1979-1982).

Pat started jumping in Texas in 1961. He helped organize and was editor for the Texas Parachute Council. He was founder and president of the University of Houston Parachute Club, with which he won the team event at the 1966 National Collegiate Parachuting Championships. He also competed with the Texas A&M team (1962-64) and Wallace's Outlaws (1964-65).

Pat lobbied successfully to include the 10-way relative work event in the National Parachuting Championships in 1972, and competed in that first 10-Way Nationals. Highlights of other competition activities include: 10-way and 4-way at the Nationals in 1978 and 1979, 8-way sequential teams Chaos (1976-77) and Element of Chance (1976), Conference Champion 4-way teams (1971-72 & 1974), the James Gang (1972-73), Godfrogs (1972) and Avis (1971).

Pat's wife, Jan, has logged more than 1400 jumps since her first in 1970. She was one of the organizers of the first all-women's SCR on the East Coast (an 11-way at Zephyrhills in 1973), and participated in several other women's records, including the first all-women's night SCR (1977) and the 24-women world record formation in 1979. She has assisted Pat in training and organization at most of his RW training camps.

Pat and Jan published the *RWUnderground* newsletter from 1972 to 1976 to promote the international growth of relative work skydiving. They also established the annual C.G. Godfrog Good Vibes Award, the RW Council's Certificates of Merit, and the annual National Champion of Combined RW Awards.

The Art of Freefall Relative Work was originally published in 1975. It has been translated in three other languages (German, French and Spanish), and adopted as a standard reference text at the U.S. Air Force Academy. Pat and Jan's other publications are *United We Fall*, a relative work anthology, and *Wings of Man: The Theory of Freefall Flight*.

GLOSSARY

Accuracy—An event in the individual competition. Each jumper attempts to land as close as possible to a 10cm target on the ground. This is considered one of two classic events.

Boogie—The term was brought back from the New Zealand International Parachuting Competition. It applies to having a great time either jumping, dancing, partying, or going away to a parachuting meet, etc.

Braking—Manipulating the steering controls and vent so as to slow or halt the forward inherent canopy speed without changing direction.

Breakoff Point—The altitude established prior to a jump whereby all jumpers stop relative work and spread out in preparation to safely open their parachutes away from one another.

Canopy Speed (Forward Speed)—The inherent horizontal speed of a canopy generated by the control of cloth porosity and the deflection of escaping air through specifically designed control or escape vents.

Dead Center—A perfect score on an accuracy jump. Each competitor attempts to touch a 10cm target as the first point of contact.

Deployment Bag—The safety device encasing the parachute canopy which (1) creates drag thereby decreasing opening chock and (2) insures that the suspension lines are fully extended prior to canopy inflation, thereby preventing jumper entanglement with the deploying canopy.

Dirt Diving—Ground practice, usually just prior to boarding the airplane. The jumpers walk through their intended maneuvers in the sequences of the actual jump. Helps develop rhythm and awareness of each persons task, as well as motivating each to do their best.

Docking—In sequential relative work, two or more formations separate and rejoin to complete a new or different formation.

Drop Zone—The open area or field surrounding the central target area designated for the landing of parachutists.

Eight Man—An event in the relative work competition. Eight jumpers have a specified amount of time to perform required formations.

Equipment Check—The final visual and physical check of the equipment made by the jumpmaster on all parachutists prior to boarding the aircraft.

Exit Point—A predetermined point on the ground over which the jumpers leave the aircraft to land in a specified area.

Experienced Parachutist—Person with over 200 parachute freefall jumps.

Four Man—An event in the relative work competition. Four jumpers have a specified amount of time to perform required formations.

Freefall—Jumping without an attachment between the parachute and the aircraft and delaying (over three seconds) the opening of the parachute. The higher the jump the longer the delay.

Funnel—In relative work, a formation collapses or breaks up by sinking from the middle. Usually caused by improper flying and too great a concentration of jumpers in one area.

Intermediate Parachutist—Person with more than 50 but less than 200 parachute freefall jumps.

Jump and Pull—Jumping and clearing the aircraft and immediately pulling the ripcord (within three seconds).

Jump Run—The final leg of flight just prior to exiting the aircraft. Varies in length based on the number exiting, type and style of aircraft, altitude, etc.

Leading Zone—The place on the airfield where the jumping list or manifest is made up and jumpers wait their turn to board the aircraft.

Log Book—The individual jump record book in which a jumper keeps a chronological record of each jump similar to a pilot's log book. Used for verifying jumping experience for licensing, competition, etc.

Malfunction—Any improper functioning of the parachute system.

Novice Parachutist—Person with less than 50 freefall parachute jumps.

Opening Altitude—2,500 feet above the ground.

Opening Shock—The tug or jerk felt by the jumper as the canopy opens and fully inflates. The degree of intensity is influenced by factors such as vertical and horizontal velocity, atmospheric condition, body position, type of parachute, method of deployment, etc. However, the standard sport parachutes in common use today contribute surprisingly little or no discomfort when properly activated.

Parachute Club—A local, autonomous, and non-commercial grouping of parachutists whos primary purpose is to enjoy the fun of parachuting. Most clubs conduct training for their own new students and may or may not be affiliated with U.S. Parachute Association.

Para Commander—An older, but highly reliable oval-shaped competition canopy of French design.

Pig Rig—Equipment worn by most relative workers. Both main and reserve parachutes are worn on the back. Also called a tandem or piggy back system.

Pilot Chute—A small spring loaded parachute which springs or leaps out into the jumpers slipstream when released by the ripcord pull. Attached to a deployment bag, it acts as dragging anchor to lift and deploy the parachute assembly until the main parachute canopy inflates.

PLF's (Parachute Landing Falls)—The method of falling down on landing by which the jumper resists, absorbs, and distributes the landing impact over various parts of the body rather than on just the feet, ankles and legs.

Pull Out Pilot Chute—A deployment device used to start the opening sequence of the main parachute. It has no spring and is usually folded in a small pouch on the jumpers waist. The pilot chute is pulled out of the pouch and held in the wind stream to inflate. Also called a throw out pilot chute.

Ram Air Parachutes—The newest designs in canopies. Rectangular in shape, it performs similar to an aircraft wing and offers a high glide ratio and speed and is very accurate for competition.

Relative Work—The cooperative aerial maneuvers executed by two or more jumpers during freefall in order to pass batons, create or "hook up" various formations, or for air-to-air photography. Such group maneuvering is tricky, due to many variables, and success is normally attained only by the more experienced parachutists.

Ripcord—The metal handle and attached steel cable and locking pins which hold the parachute closed until the jumper pulls it loose, thereby unlocking the pack and freeing the pilot chute and canopy to deploy.

Sequential R/W—A popular form of skydiving where groups of jumpers build different formations in the sky in a particular sequence. Oftentimes these formations are separate and flown back together again.

Skygod—A term to describe relative work jumpers who talk better than they jump. Usually a close cousin of a whuffo.

Sport Parachuting (Sky Diving or Jumping)—The art of exiting from an aircraft over the proper point at a high altitude, stabilizing the body during a free or delayed fall, executing various controlled body maneuvers—either alone or with others—safely opening the parachute at a given time and point, and then controlling the parachute so as to land safely on a specific ground target.

Spotting—The technique of selecting the course to fly, directing the pilot, dropping the wind drift indicator, selecting the correct ground reference point over which to (1) exit from the aircraft and (2) open the parachute.

Star—A term which is applied to a hook-up of 5 or more jumpers holding each others' wrists. The formation which is achieved resembles a star from the ground.

Steering Lines (Toggles, Knobs)—The special lines and their handles which are attached to key control panels and vents to "drive" the parachute canopy by controlling the angle and shape of the vents which affect the horizontal and vertical canopy speed and the direction.

Style—An event in the individual competition. Each jumper has 25 seconds to do a series of 360° turns and loops. The competitors are judged on time and headings. This is considered one of two classic events.

Ten Man—Often referred to as the 100 yd. dash of relative work. Ten skydivers exit an airplane and form a round circle in the fastest time.

Terminal Velocity—The greatest speed at which a body falls through the atmosphere (176 feet per second or 120 m.p.h.), which is constant after the 12th second of freefall.

Trac—A competitive event combining accuracy and relative work. A team of four jumpers perform various maneuvers in freefall and land on a predetermined target. The team is judged on time and total distance.

United States Parachute Association (USPA)—The only national sport parachuting organization in the United States dedicated solely to the promotion, improvement, and safety of parachuting and the parachutist. It also selects and trains the United States Parachute Team and enters it into international and world championship competition.

Whuffo—The term now generally applied to non-jumping spectators. The term originated earlier in agricultural areas when curious farmers paused in their work to inquire, "Whuffo you-all jump outta them pair-chutes?"

Wind Line—An imaginary wind direction line extending from the true opening point to the target center. Such lines vary in direction and velocity at different altitudes. The accuracy competitor attempts to stay on this wind line until he touches the target.

Wind Streamer—A narrow length of colored and weighted paper or cloth dropped prior to the start of jumping to measure wind speed and direction to assist in selecting the proper exit and opening point. The indicator has approximately the same rate of descent as a parachutist with an open canopy.

ZAP—Zero All Points. Occurs when a competitor or team makes enough mistakes which causes a loss of all points.

Mike Horan

Team Chaos.   *M. Anderson Jenkins.*

Team Chaos.   *M. Anderson Jenkins.*

MANEUVERS
SECTION

INTRODUCTION

All maneuvers and sequential relative work start with a hook-up. This hook-up is the key to the rest of the maneuver. There are five basic hook-ups:

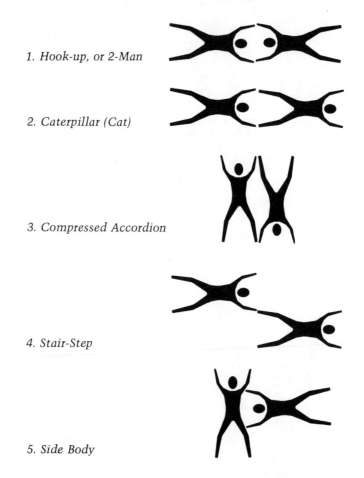

1. *Hook-up, or 2-Man*

2. *Caterpillar (Cat)*

3. *Compressed Accordion*

4. *Stair-Step*

5. *Side Body*

The possible combinations which can be built from these fundamental hook-ups are limited only by your skill and imagination.

Fig. 1.
THE BI-POLE (2 Methods)

Method 1:

a.	*b.*	*c.*
3-man compressed accordion. Wing men fold-out to present legs to *.	* Enters	Bi-Pole

Method 2:

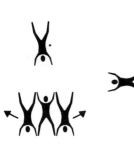 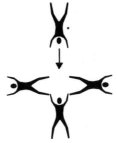 

a.	*b.*	*c.*
* Enters on legs of a 2-man line to form base. At *'s signal, # fold-out to present legs to 4.	4 Enters	* Backs out to form bi-pole

Fig. 2.

DONUT (How to Build a Donut)+

a.
Base. Simultaneously, each flyer puts his left hand on his own left knee. This allows each flyer to grab the proffered knee with his right hand.

b.
Flyers put hand to knee—grip change. Look into the center-switch on signal.

c.
Change grips to get right hand outboard. Hold hand above head to stop spinning; look into the center—fly.

Fig. 3.

DONUT DOUBLE FLAKE

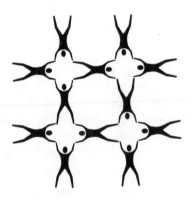

a.
Maneuver built from a donut base.

+For alternate method of building a donut, see Fig. #5(a-c).

Fig. 4.

BI-POLE TO A DONUT

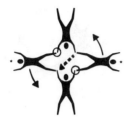

a.
Bi-pole base, drop grips at
*o; * fold out to form (b).*

b.
Double compressed
*accordion. * grab leg.*

c.
Drop grip o; # grip
change.

d.
Donut

(0 = break grip)

Fig. 5.

MULTIPLE 4-MAN MANEUVERS (ONE JUMP)

a.
Compressed accordion
base.

b.
Opposed diamond

c.
Grip-switch to donut.

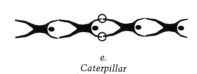

e.
Caterpillar

d.
Drop grip and fold-out to
(e).

f.
Drop grip to form two
2-caterpillars. Switch
grips to form (g.).

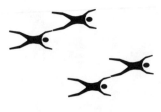

g.
Left hand stair-steps.

h.
Left hand stair-steps.
Dock into facing
diamond.

Fig. 6.
SEQUENTIAL 5-DOUBLE DONUT

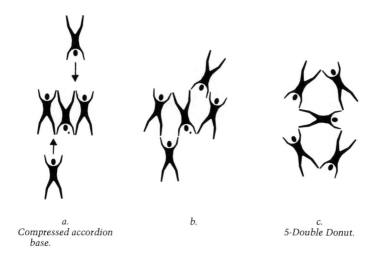

a.
Compressed accordion
base.

b.

c.
5-Double Donut.

Fig. 7.
4-MAN MANEUVER SET

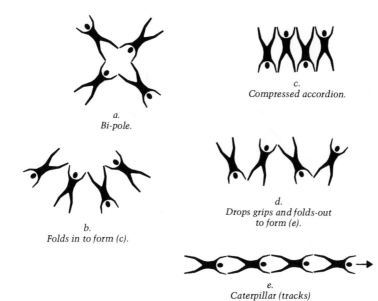

a.
Bi-pole.

c.
Compressed accordion.

b.
Folds in to form (c).

d.
Drops grips and folds-out
to form (e).

e.
Caterpillar (tracks)

Fig. 8.
BI-FLAKED BI-POLE

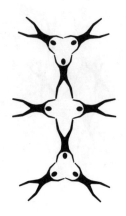

Fig. 9.
TRIPOD

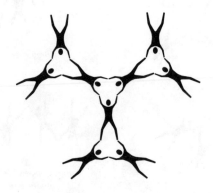

Fig. 10.
9-CLUSTER

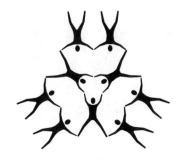

Fig. 11.
12-CLUSTER

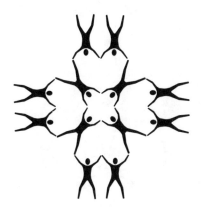

Fig. 12.
TRI-DIAMONDS

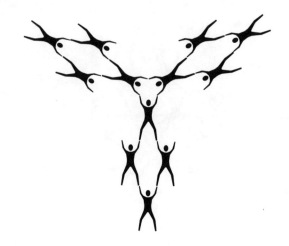

Fig. 13.
EAGLE TO FRENCH CONNECTION

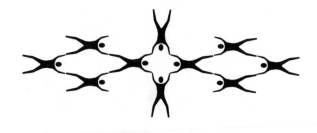

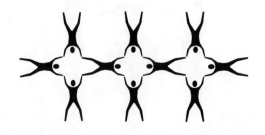

Fig. 14.
EAGLE (Variation)

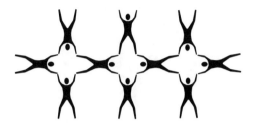

Fig. 15.
THE WEDGE

Fig. 16.
HOUR GLASS

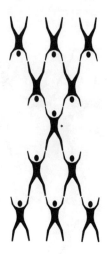

Fig. 17.
9-DIAMOND

* *Good pull-out*

Fig. 18.
TRIPLE DIAMONDS

Fig. 19.
TRIPLE HORIZONTAL DIAMONDS

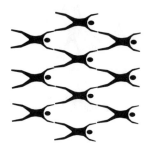

Fig. 20.

SEQUENCE DOUBLE DIAMOND TO FOUR POINT SNOWFLAKE

a.
Double Diamond to:

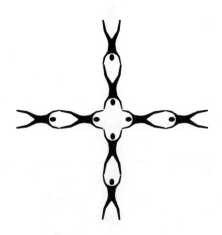

b.
4-Point Snowflake.

Fig. 21.

JAMES GANG
SPEED STAR MANEUVER "A"
(Involves a Lot of Flying)

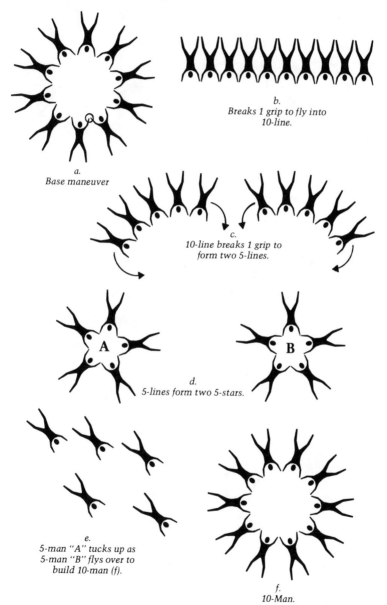

b.
Breaks 1 grip to fly into
10-line.

a.
Base maneuver

c.
10-line breaks 1 grip to
form two 5-lines.

d.
5-lines form two 5-stars.

e.
5-man "A" tucks up as
5-man "B" flys over to
build 10-man (f).

f.
10-Man.

Fig. 22.

ALL STARS SPEED STAR MANEUVER "B"

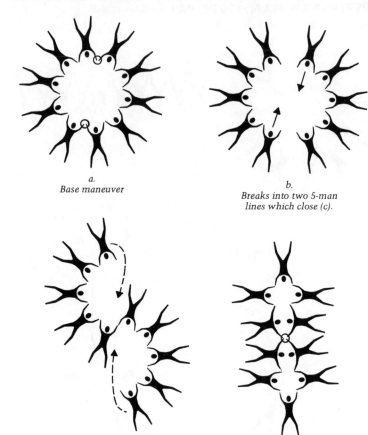

a.
Base maneuver

b.
Breaks into two 5-man
lines which close (c).

c.
"S"-line closes ends in.

d.
Closed double lines.

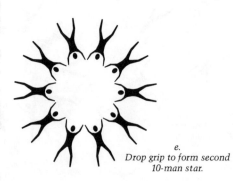

(0 = break grip)

e.
Drop grip to form second
10-man star.

Fig. 23.

DARE TO BE GREAT
(A 10-Man Sequence Involving a Lot of Flying)

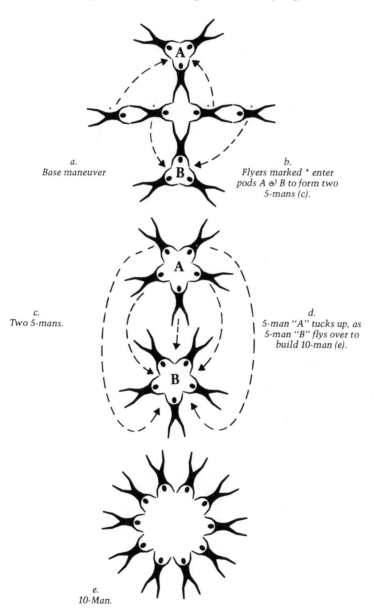

a.
Base maneuver

b.
Flyers marked * enter
pods A & B to form two
5-mans (c).

c.
Two 5-mans.

d.
5-man "A" tucks up, as
5-man "B" flys over to
build 10-man (e).

e.
10-Man.

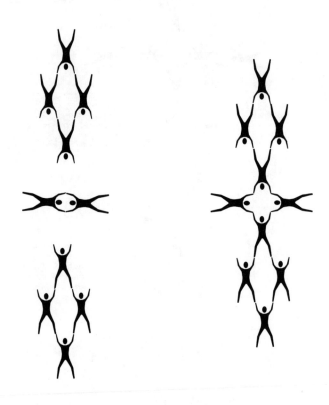

Fig. 24.

**DOUBLE DIAMOND DOCK TO FORM
AN EAGLE**

Fig. 25.

THE 8-MAN IN-OUT (How to Do It)

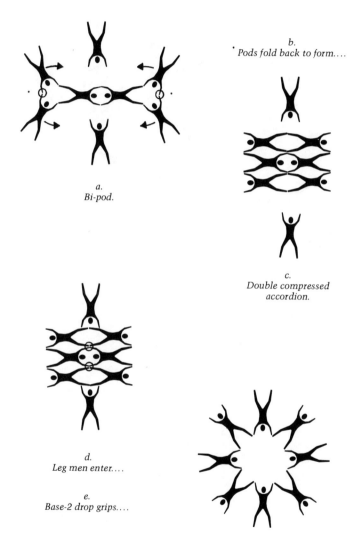

a.
Bi-pod.

b.
Pods fold back to form....

c.
Double compressed
accordion.

d.
Leg men enter....

e.
Base-2 drop grips....

f.
The 8-man in-out.

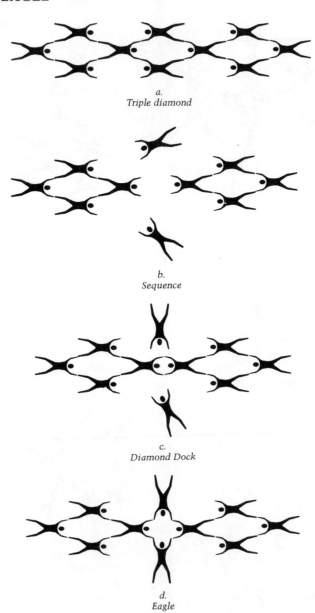

Fig. 26.

SEQUENTIAL MANEUVER:
TRIPLE DIAMOND TO DIAMOND DOCK TO FORM
AN EAGLE

a.
Triple diamond

b.
Sequence

c.
Diamond Dock

d.
Eagle

Fig. 27.
16-MAN DIAMOND

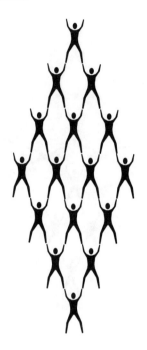

Fig. 28.
16-MAN QUADRAPOD

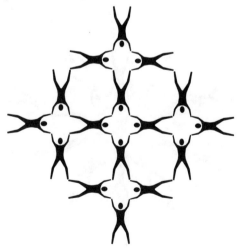

Fig. 29.
16-MAN QUADRA-DIAMOND

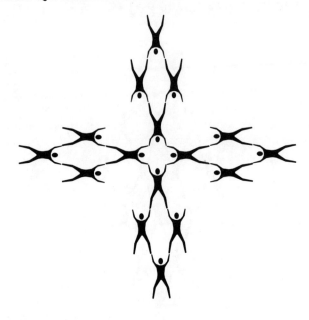

Fig. 30.
20-MAN SNOWFLAKE

ACKNOWLEDGEMENTS

The author would like to acknowledge the many people whose thoughts and ideas have contributed to this book.

The Art of Freefall Relative Work deals with the technique of perfection and the attitude of joy, i.e. flight for the joy of flying. These are esoteric thoughts...subtle in character, difficult to describe, hard to communicate. To produce the clearest statement on the art of skydiving, I embraced all that I had ever heard, experienced or seen relating to perfection and joy.

In formulating my approach to flight for the joy of flying, I used the works of the *Vedas*, the *Upanishads*, Hesse's *Sidhartha*, the books of Carlos Castenada and of Richard Brautigan, the excellent works of W.Y. Evans-Wentz (notably *The Tibetan Book of the Dead* and *The Book of the Great Liberation*), Baba Ram Dass' *Be Here Now* Swami Sri Yukteswar's *The Holy Science*, William James' *Pragmatism*, the writings of Richard Bach, various tests on philisopy, M. Murphy, *Intellectual Digest*, many other people and books too numerous to mention, but especially the Swami Prabhavananda translation of the *Bhagavad-Gita.*

In describing the technique of pefect flight, I am deeply indebted to Jerry Bird, Jim Bohr, Carlos Wallace, Red Kosteba, Stan Troeller, Gruber Gorman, Skratch Garrison, Matt Farmer, B.J. Worth, Rande Deluca, Roger Hull, Kevin Shea, the Greene County jumpers, Ed Fitch, Clyde Jacks, our freefall photographers, and many more. Also, Denis Jenkinson's *The Racing Driver*, Colin Campbell's *The Sports Car: Its Design and Performance*, my yoga teachers, my fencing masters, Pietro Trauffiris' *The Technique of Motor Racing*, and particularly Wolfgang Langewiesch's outstanding text on flying, *Stick and Rudder*, provided excellent technical input.

The real acknowledgement is to my sky-mates on good skydives, teammates from some 15-20 teams, competitors from 16+ years of parachute meets...I acknowledge gratefully and with immense pleasure all the hours of freefall relative work we've shared, and will reshare with those who come later.

Madden Travis "Pat" Works, Jr.

MAKING THE DIVE
Collected Helpful Hints

Pick maneuvers that match the ability of those on the load.

Encourage no-contact as a fast way to learn awareness and perfect flight.

Determine positions. Use some of the more experienced people who can build a fast, solid base up front. Use less experienced flyers on the outside edges.

Design an exit which is as fast and efficient as possible. Plan to use floaters.

Gear up and walk through the dive on the ground from exit to break-off at least two or three times. Make sure everyone knows what to do.

Practice exit before takeoff.

Exit as fast and close together as possible.

Build large maneuvers in waves or stages, i.e. in a donut-flake, the flakers should set up and wait until the base is *complete and stable.* Don't enter your slot until your counterpart on the other side of the formation can enter theirs. Never add float or sink to the formation.

Perfect speed is being at the right place at the right time. Perfect speed is being *there* so as to mesh with the flow of the developing dive smoothly.

Always take leg grips at the knee or thigh; never interfere with another's key control surfaces.

All docking should be done so that no momentum is transmitted into the formation.

Some formations float. Anticipate this. Don't go low.

Concentrate on your flying assignment with happy abandon. If everyone does, it will go.

Although our medium is air—don't forget the ground. Those in the base formation must cross-reference the ground to keep the formation from turning or sliding.

When flying formations, all members must fly smoothly and united. For example, in a diamond fly as smoothly as you would fly on your own. Don't over-fly your part. The point man on a diamond initiates turns by bending at the waist toward the direction desired. Braking is primarily the job of the tail person Anticipate the necessary corrections—be smooth and deliberate.

Don't try to salvage a bad approach by hanging on and swinging or climbing your man's legs, etc. Let go and fly back into the formation.

As soon as practical after landing, regroup and walk through the jump as it happened. Analyze and correct mistakes. Emphasize the maneuvers that went well. Use tact.

Think together, fly together, and your whole scene will flow together.

Team Chaos.   *M. Anderson Jenkins.*

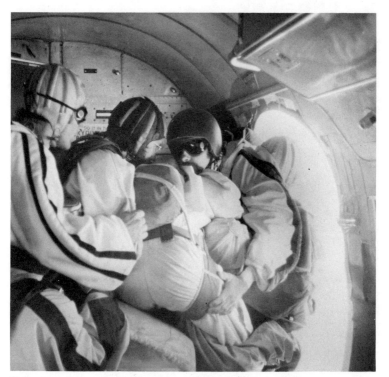

Exitus Line-up.

The Exit-1.   *Kevin Shea.*

The Exit-2. *Kevin Shea.*

THE ART OF FREEFALL RELATIVE WORK clearly sets forth the techniques of flying. It represents 15 years of experience and four years of research and writing. In vivid detail and in unique original drawings it describes how masterful relative work is done.

Andy Keech

Andy Keech

Ray Cottingham